0

LEADING THE WAY

Black Women in Canada

by

Rosemary Sadlier

Umbrella Press
56 Rivercourt Boulevard
Toronto, On. M4J 3A4

DEDICATION

This book is dedicated to my late father, Henry Albert Sadlier, and my mother, Bernice W. Sadlier, for their examples of strength and determination; and to my husband, Dr. Jay Carey, and our children, Jenne, Raia and Alexander for their patience, encouragement and support.

LEADING THE WAY: Black Women In Canada

Publisher:	Kenneth H. Pearson
Editorial:	Jocelyn Smyth
	Lesli Pearson
Concept Design:	The Design Group
Design and Layout:	Becker Associates
Cover Art:	Stephen Taylor

Canadian Cataloguing in Publication Data
Sadlier, Rosemary
Leading the way: Black women in Canada

Includes bibliographical references and index.
ISBN 1-895642-11-6

1. Women, Black - Canada - Biography. I. Title.

FC106.B6S3 1994 305.48'896071 C94-930411-5
F1035.N3S3 1994

Printed and Bound in Canada
1 2 3 4 5 6 7 8 9 0 / 4 5 6 7 8 9 0 1 2 3

Publisher

UMBRELLA PRESS
56 Rivercourt Blvd.
Toronto, ON. M4J 3A4
Telephone: (416) 696 6665
Fax: (416) 696 9189

CONTENTS

PREFACE

I believe that every individual has the potential to make a difference, to lead the way, to promote positive and productive changes in society through their talent, hard work, dedication, courage, decisiveness and commitment. The Black women included in this book are but a sample of the purposeful women of African descent in Canada and they represent a range of abilities from across the country and extend over generations. I decided to select women who were internationally, nationally and locally known and possess diverse abilities to increase the possibility that the reader might identify with a familiar individual or gain a greater understanding of the achievements of Black women in Canada.

This book was born of my experiences speaking to students about Black history. I came to realize how important Black role models were in providing a complete picture of the contributions of Canadians of all colours and in enhancing racial pride. It is my hope that young people will be encouraged to follow the steps taken by these women, knowing that their chosen road may have been travelled by others or that improved race relations or a deeper appreciation of Canadian cultural diversity will result.

As I researched and wrote this book, many people, who were committed to ensuring the publication of a helpful educational reference, assisted me. This assistance took many forms - from the women who were interviewed and included in the book, to the resource people who were consulted. Many people rearranged their schedules to assist me because they were interested in seeing this book published.

I would like to extend my gratitude to everyone who assisted me and, in particular, a special thanks to Jean Augustine, Dr. Carrie Best, Dr. Rosemary Brown, John Desmond, Beverley Mascoll, Anne Packwood, Mairuth Sarsfield and Sylvia Sweeney for the time they made available to me for our interviews. And thanks to Aileen Williams who typed the initial drafts of the manuscript and offered valuable suggestions.

In addition to the women who have shared their time, biographies and pictures with me, I wish to thank the following people for their generous assistance which has helped to make this book possible: Genevieve Balogun, Calgary; Henry Bishop, Halifax; Wilson Brooks, Toronto; Don Carty, Toronto; Cynthia Darrell, Toronto; Dolly Glasgow-Williams, Halifax; the late Dr. Wilson Head, Toronto; Nolie Herbert, Toronto; Dr. Daniel Hill, Toronto; Dr. Rodney Leacock, Halifax; Reverend Jean Markham, Toronto; Alice Newby, North Buxton; Lyda Peters, Montreal; Gwen Robinson, Chatham; Grace Skeir, Halifax; Clifford Skinner, Saint John. I am also grateful for the resources of the St. Catharines Public Library, the Ontario Black History Society, the Moorland-Springarn Resource Center of Howard University, Washington, D.C. and the Black Community Centre of Dartmouth, Nova Scotia.

This book was made possible by financial assistance from Canadian Heritage.

Rosemary Sadlier
Toronto, On.
February, 1994

HARRIET TUBMAN

Moses of Her People

BORN: 1820 Bucktown, Maryland
DEATH: March 10, 1913 Auburn, New York

HARRIET WAS BORN A SLAVE, the fourth generation of her family to be used as slaves in the United States. Short, plain and the victim of a beating that caused sudden sleeping spells, she was spared the typical fate of many young enslaved women. Instead of being sold away from her family or forced to have children who would also become slaves, she was able to build up her strength by doing hard work usually performed by male slaves. She was also able to learn about surviving and traveling away from the plantation which would later serve her well as she led others to freedom.

With determination and courage, Harriet first set out on her own for freedom in the northern United States and successfully made herself "free". Not satisfied with her own liberty, she made a total of 19 trips to slave-holding areas in the South, guiding over 300 enslaved people to their freedom. Eleven of her rescues saw her deliver her "passengers" to St. Catharines, Ontario. Through her courage and commitment, Harriet became one of the most successful "conductors" on the Underground Railroad. Although not formally educated, in her later life she became an effective speaker throughout the northern United States and spoke on the need for emancipation and on women's rights.

EARLY LIFE

Harriet was born on the Brodess plantation in Dorchester County, Maryland and she was the youngest of eleven children of Ben and Harriet ("Rit") Green Ross. As a young child, she was allowed to run about the plantation while older family members worked either on the plantation or at neighbouring plantations. She quickly came to despise slavery as she saw her playmates and later her sisters, Sophy and Linah, sold to raise money for their master. Slaves had no rights, neither over themselves nor rights over their children. Because slaves were regarded as property, they were not taught to read nor write, nor allowed to travel without permission. In fact, slaves were not allowed to do anything, except what the owner wanted them to do. Once a slave in the New World, there were few means of becoming freed. There were, however, times when slaves were set free, such as through the last will and testament of their owner, which was called manumission, or by making a run for liberty to a free or non-slave state, which was called self-emancipation.

Harriet Tubman

Harriet's days of playtime were over by the age of five when she was hired out. Without being given any instructions, Harriet was told to dust and sweep a room. She did this but because the woman who hired her from her master was not satisfied with her work, she beat Harriet around her face and neck after each of Harriet's four attempts to clean the room. Until the day she died, Harriet bore the scars of these and other beatings. Harriet was also expected to hold the master's baby for hours to keep the baby from crying all night. Harriet was shown how to weave, but the fibers in the air bothered her and instead of being forced to weave she was sent to tend the muskrat traps in the nearby swamp. With the dampness and the insects of the swamp, Harriet became ill but was forced to continue tending the traps to the point of collapse. Slaves were not allowed to be attended by a doctor and she was sent back to her mother, Rit, to be cared for. Slaves were not considered people and, therefore, had to develop their own ways of getting well, instead of being cared for by a doctor.

MANUMISSION

By law, the captured Africans brought to the New World as slaves were not considered to have status as people. As a slave, you were prevented by law from owning anything, including yourself. As a slave on the plantations in the United States, you were regarded only in terms of the work you were expected to do much like animals on the plantation. However, some slave owners would grant a slave freedom and ownership of him or herself, called "manumission". A slave was granted freedom by the master through the slave owner's last will and testament for various reasons, such as a recognition of the loyalty of the slave through the years of servitude, because a slave was too old to sell profitably or possibly through the master's fear of not getting into heaven if a higher power was opposed to slavery.

By the time Harriet was nine years old, her inability in traditional slave women's work convinced Brodess to try Harriet at something else. Even at a young age, she hated to be under the constant glare of household supervisors. She was hired out to do the same tasks, splitting rails and hauling logs, as her father. While doing this, she learned practical ways of the wild that would help her later. She learned to tell which direction is north from the way moss grows on trees, or by following the Choptank River as it flowed west into the northerly flowing Chesapeake, or from the position of the Big Dipper, known as the "Drinking Gourd", in the night sky. While Harriet's owner may have been "fair", in comparison with other slave owners, he did treat his slaves harshly, particularly when he developed financial problems. To raise money, he abruptly decided to sell two of Harriet's sisters, Linah and Sophy. This act not only separated the sisters from their family but also meant that two of Linah's and Sophy's children had to be left behind. This was not unusual for slaves as they had no control over their lives. Harriet decided that she would do everything she could to take control of her life and seek her freedom.

THE DRINKING GOURD

Slaves were constantly being watched and listened to because overseers wanted to maintain control over them. To be able to speak without fear, coded messages were used. Sometimes a song or phrase would have one meaning for outsiders and a different significance for Blacks. The Big Dipper was called the "Drinking Gourd" and signified the freedom that could be had by following it to freedom in the free states of the North or to Canada.

THE CALL FOR FREEDOM

In 1835, Harriet saw a slave named Jim make a run for his freedom and she was ordered to help recapture him. She found Jim in a Bucktown store but instead of telling the masters where he was she allowed Jim to escape while she blocked the door from the searchers trying to go after him. Furious at her action, a two-pound weight was thrown at her by the overseer, hitting her in the forehead. Harriet would have died, except for the nursing care of her mother. However, as a result of this injury, she was affected for the rest of her life by sudden sleep attacks. When Harriet was able to return to work months later, she was only permitted to keep a very small part of her wages, which she used to buy oxen to assist her travelling, even though most slaves were not usually permitted to buy or own anything. Harriet's determination to be free continued to grow.

There was one of two things that I have a right to:
liberty or death.
If I could not have one, I could have the other
for no man should take me alive.
I shall fight for my liberty and when the time comes
for me to go, the Lord will let them take me.

In 1844 Harriet married John Tubman, a Black man who had been freed through the manumission granted to his mother. She began to explore her own mother's status as a slave and discovered that, in fact, her mother too had been declared free but had not been told of her freedom. Because she was Rit's daughter, Harriet knew, therefore, that she too should be a free person, and she became even more determined to escape and live in liberty. However, her husband, John Tubman, would not think of escaping north with her and, in fact, threatened to alert her master if she were to try to escape. Harriet knew that her plans had to be kept secret even from her husband because he would not support her dream.

On March 9, 1849, Harriet's owner, Brodess, died leaving his possessions, including his slaves, to his wife, who had little interest in farming and keeping the slaves. Harriet learned that Mrs. Brodess was going to sell her and her brothers further south. She immediately formed a plan to escape. At first, Harriet set out with her brothers, but their fear of recapture and the probable consequences was greater than their need to be free, so Harriet

Stockholders
of the Underground
R.R. Company
Hold on to Your Stock!!

The market has an upward tendency. By the express train which arrived this morning at 3 o'clock, fifteen thousand dollars worth of human merchandise, consisting of twenty-nine able-bodied men and women, fresh and sound, from the Carolina and Kentucky plantations, have arrived safe at the depot on the other side, where all our sympathising colonization friends may have an opportunity of expressing their sympathy by bringing forward donations of ploughs, etc., farming utensils, pick axes and hoes, and not old clothes; as these emigrants all can till the soil.
N.B. Stockholders don't forget the meeting to-day at 2 o'clock at the ferry on the Canada side. All persons desiring to take stock in this prosperous company, be sure to be on hand.

Detroit, April 19, 1853

By Order of the
BOARD OF DIRECTORS[12]

THE UNDERGROUND RAILROAD

The Underground Railroad was neither below ground nor a railroad. In fact, it was not a single mode of transportation as those using it travelled by foot, cart, buggy, horseback, boat, over land and water to get to their destination. It was a secret system of people-helping-people to attain freedom from slavery by providing aid to slaves on their escapes to the free states in the north, or all the way to Canada. The organization of the Underground Railroad operated secretly or in an "underground " way because the penalties for helping a person in bondage were severe for both those helping the escaping slaves, the abolitionists, and the freedom-seeking slave. The network of people willing to put their own lives at risk for what they believed to be unfair, slavery, was so efficient that some suspected that an actual train existed to rush fugitives out of slave holding areas. The actual means of transportation was on foot, sometimes, when hidden or with disguises, by wagon, boat or train. Both Black and White abolitionists were committed to ending slavery and doing what they could to assist slaves to become free people.

The Underground Railroad may have started as early 1800, with the passage of the first Fugitive Slave law in the United States in 1793, but it was firmly established following the War of 1812 when Canada was publicized as a safe place for slaves. The North ignored the law of 1793 and a system known as the Underground Railroad was started to help fugitives to escape to Canada. The Quakers, a religious group, were among the first people to aid the freedom seekers but many others joined as the abolitionist movement became more influential. With the passage of the second Fugitive Slave Act in 1850, which required all citizens to co-operate in enforcement of the new law and requiring that captured runaway slaves be brought before a federal court without consitutional protection of the individual, all Blacks were at risk. In the northern states the law aroused bitter opposition, leading to defiance of the law. On June 28, 1864, the Fugitive Slave Law was finally repealed by Congress of the United States, and following the Civil War there was no longer a need for the organized escape routes known as the Underground Railroad.

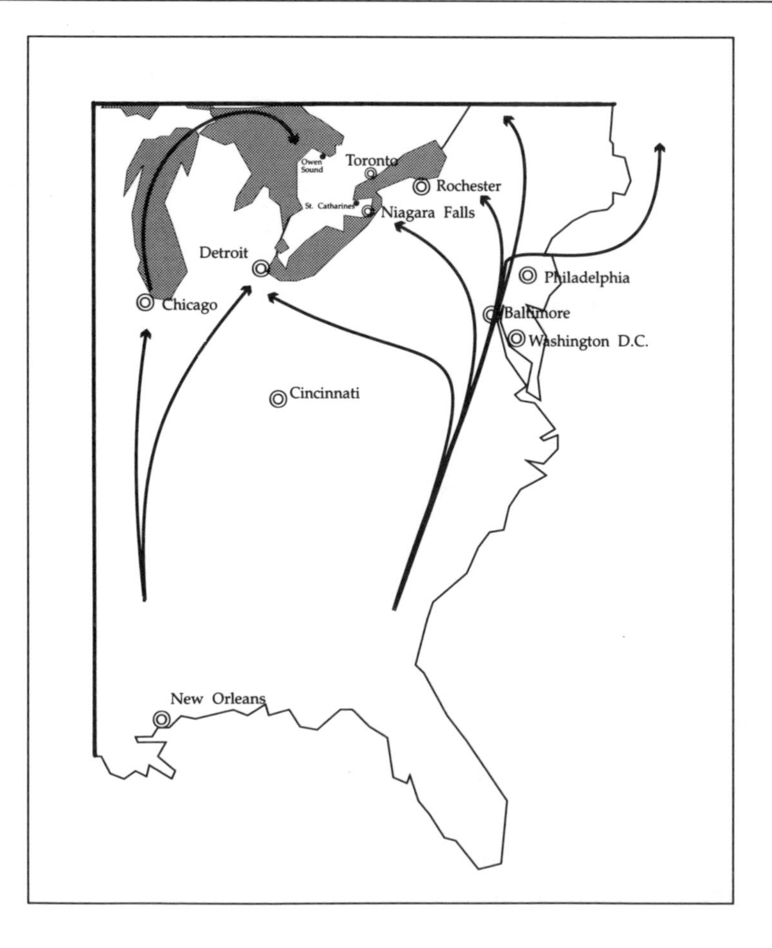

had to return with them to the Brodess plantation. She was determined to escape and two days later she started out again, but this time on her own. She travelled by night and slept by day and was able to get food or short rides with the Quakers and others who opposed slavery and were willing to help escaping slaves. By her own courage, determination and strength she finally reached Philadelphia and her freedom. Her escape on the Underground Railroad took several weeks and Harriet was already thinking about making a return trip to get her husband and family. She was now free and Harriet wanted to see all of her people living in freedom.

QUAKERS

Members of this pacifist or peace-promoting religious order, also known as the Society of Friends, were strongly opposed to slavery and may have felt forced to respond to the brutal treatment of slaves who were seeking their freedom. The Friends established the first anti-slavery society in the United States as early as 1775. Many members of the Quaker religion were involved with the Underground Railroad and they provided many safe houses and assisted fugitive slaves in areas where they lived and worshipped, particularly in Pennsylvania.

One of the first people Harriet wanted to rescue was her sister Mary Ann Bowley. Harriet didn't know how to write so she asked someone to write a letter to Mary Ann's husband, John Bowley, who was a free man and could read. Through this letter, Harriet advised John that if he could bring Mary Ann as far north as Baltimore she would conduct Mary Ann on to Philadelphia. Unfortunately, the plan had to be changed at the last minute because of the sudden decision of Mary Ann's master to sell her at a slave auction. Harriet rushed to the site of the slave auction and, while the bidding for Mary Ann was taking place, Harriet took Mary Ann to a safe hiding place. Later, she led her to freedom in a wagon with six horses.

Families were often separated by slave auctions.

For her next rescue, Harriet sought out her brother John Ross, but in his escape he had to leave without his wife and sons as his wife had been sold away and his sons could not leave the owners' house. Later, John Bowley was able to assist Harriet and her brother by travelling as a freeperson into Talbot County, Maryland, where he rescued John Ross's sons and brought them to their father. These first rescues were successful and gave Harriet the confidence to attempt to conduct others to freedom.

LEVI COFFIN

Coffin was born in North Carolina but later moved to Cincinnati. He was a Quaker who made his home in Cincinnati a major hiding place and refuge for over one hundred freedom-seeking refugee slaves a year. Coffin became known as the "President" of the Underground Railroad for his efficiency in handling the precious "cargo", people that he assisted.

In the fall of 1851, Harriet returned to Bucktown to bring her husband north to her home in Philadelphia where they could live together in freedom. Surprisingly, she discovered that he had taken another wife and he was not interested in going to Philadelphia with her. Harriet was shocked and terribly disappointed. As a "fugitive" slave, there was nothing she could do but accept the fact. She decided to use the trip as an opportunity to signal to others, through familiar Negro Spirituals, that she was seeking passengers to go North on her freedom train. On this mission, Harriet brought back ten freedom seekers to liberty in Philadelphia. However, when the Fugitive Slave Act was passed in 1850, even Blacks who had been freed and were living in "free" states could be recaptured and put back into slavery. This law made it possible for anyone to accuse any Black person of being a fugitive anywhere in the United States, thereby sending the accused back to the South as a slave. This inhumane law affected even those who had never been enslaved and who managed to be educated and prosper in the free states.

THE FUGITIVE SLAVE ACT OF 1850

The Fugitive Slave Act of 1850 made it legal for anyone, anywhere in the United States to accuse any Black person of being an escaped slave. This law put dark-skinned Caucasians at risk as well. The claim was then processed by a lone judge who would make more money if he ruled in favour of the slave holder. This second Fugitive Slave Act was passed to appease the interests of the slave-holding south who accused the northern free states of harbouring runaways since the passage of the weaker Fugitive Slave Act of 1793.

When Harriet rescued her brother James Ross, his family and nine others, she headed for safety in British-controlled Canada, where slavery had been abolished in 1834. She made St. Catharines headquarters for herself and the slave refugees and rented a home at the corner of Geneva and North Street, near the British Methodist

ABOLITION OF SLAVERY IN THE BRITISH EMPIRE

The British Imperial Act of 1833 abolished slavery, effective August 1,1834, throughout the British Empire, which included Canada. This end to slavery came after decades of measures proposed by abolitionists designed to slow the slave trade to the New World and elsewhere.

THE UNDERGROUND RAILROAD TERMS

Railway terms were used to confuse slave catchers. The following were some of the common terms:

STATION: Sometimes known as a "Depot". A safe resting point where the escaping slaves could rest with some sense of security, perhaps a root cellar, a hidden room, a church belfry or a barn. Stations were often 25 to 30 km. apart.

STATION MASTER: Sometimes known as "Agent". The person who would guard and provide food or clothing to the hiding or resting freedom seekers.

CONDUCTOR: The person who would lead a group of slaves along a section of the escape route or all the way to freedom.

PASSENGER: Sometimes called "Cargo", "Freight" or "Package", were brave and determined Black people who were escaping bondage with the help of the Underground Railroad

STOCKHOLDERS: People who assisted freedom seekers by donating money, food or clothing to the network.

TERMINAL: The final destination of the freedom seekers.

Episcopal Church of Canada, which still stands today, and where she worshipped. At that time, St. Catharines was a significant centre for Black settlement with 1000 Blacks out of a population of 7000, and her home was located in the centre of the Black section of St. Catharines. Many Blacks had made the Niagara peninsula-Niagara Falls, Niagara-On-The-Lake their home, following their service as Loyalists during the American War of Independence in the previous century, or as recruits and enlistees during the War of 1812 and the Mackenzie Rebellions of 1837, as well as freedom seekers from slavery in the United States. Some Blacks had been given land grants as war veterans and others had a continuing interest in defending the Canadian border, while others had favourable work opportunities, such as building the Welland Canal, working in hotels, clearing land and building roads. Harriet's decision to make St. Catharines her headquarters was influenced by the short distance across the Niagara River separating the slave-supporting United States and the freedom that was possible in Canada. Because of this, she would be able to keep the travel time of her "Freedom Train", the Underground Railroad, to a minimum. Harriet lived in St. Catharines with her family until 1858 when she moved to Auburn, New York, to live in her own country.

TO BE SOLD,

A BLACK WOMAN, named PEGGY, aged about forty years ; and a Black boy her ſon, named JUPITER, aged about fifteen years, both of them the property of the Subſcriber.

The Woman is a tolerable Cook and waſher woman and perfectly underſtands making Soap and Candles.

The Boy is tall and ſtrong of his age, and has been employed in Country buſineſs, but brought up principally as a Houſe Servant—They are each of them Servants for life. The Price for the Wowan is one hundred and fifty Dollars—for the Boy two hundred Dollars, payable in three years with Intereſt from the day of Sale and to be properly ſecured by Bond &c.—But one fourth leſs will be taken in ready Money.

PETER RUSSELL.

York, Feb. 10th 1806.

Notice in the Upper Canada Gazette

Through Underground Railroad contacts, Harriet learned that her brothers, who remained in the South, were to be sold on December 26, 1854, and she quickly went to their aid. Harriet's brothers Benjamin, Henry and Robert, and three others, met Harriet near their parents' cabin so that they could say farewell to their father before heading north. Slaves who ran away, and often those who assisted them, were often beaten, maimed or killed as a lesson to others. The freedom seekers decided not to contact their mother because they thought she would be so excited to know that Harriet was there that she would not be able to contain herself. To protect their father from having to tell those searching for Harriet that she had been there, he was blindfolded so he would be able to say honestly that he had not seen Harriet nor any of the freedom seekers.

from the St. Catharines Historical Museum

Harriet was dedicated to bringing Blacks to Canada and the slave-owning population of Maryland was just as committed to capturing Harriet. During one rescue mission in 1859, Harriet found that slave owners in Maryland had offered a reward of $40,000, equivalent to about $250 million today, for her arrest because of the assistance she gave to the freedom seekers.

> **"FREE" STATE**
> A "free" state was any state north of the Mason-Dixon line, the boundary between Pennsylvania and Maryland, the boundary between northern Union states and the southern Confederate states where slave-holding was not permitted by law. "Free" states came into being by 1777 and included Maine, Vermont, New Hampshire, New York and Pennsylvania. Freedom seekers settled in these northern states until the passing of the Fugitive Slave Act put their freedom at risk. The Maritimes, Quebec and Ontario then became locations that attracted freedom seekers.

Her rescues were always made in the spring and fall of the year. To finance these escapes, she would save her money from her summer and winter employment, as well as the assistance from the Anti-Slavery Society of Canada and the American Missionary Association. Most of her trips were made at night with only the North Star to guide her. The road to a new life free of slavery was long and some freedom seekers escaping with Harriet questioned her ability to deliver them to the "Promised Land". When she did lead them to freedom, they called her "Moses" after the biblical figure who freed the slaves in ancient times. Harriet was not always gentle with the freedom seekers and was known to threaten anyone who wanted to turn back with the phrase, "Live North or die here!", while holding a pistol. Rightly, she believed that just one former slave turning back would put the whole group in a dangerous position since slave catchers would readily be able to narrow their area of search and increase the chances of catching them. Even when disguises were used, discretion and secrecy were critical to the success of Harriet's escapes.

Children if you are tired, keep going;
if you are scared, keep going;
if you are hungry, keep going;
if you want to taste freedom, keep going.

John Brown

THE AMERICAN CIVIL WAR AND AFTER

Harriet was well known to individual abolitionists who often provided financial assistance for Underground Railroad travels and rescues, as did Canadian and American anti-slavery groups. She was a participant in their social functions and came to know powerful people who shared her vision of equality and dignity for all people. She met and supported John Brown who led the attack on Harper's Ferry, and she would have been with him at Harper's Ferry had she not become ill. Harriet credited Brown even more than the President of the United States, Abraham Lincoln, for seeking to end that "peculiar institution", slavery. Harriet had worked

closely with an abolitionist, Thomas Garrett, when she lived in Philadelphia and Frederick Douglass, a self-emancipated Black man, who was a leader of the abolitionist movement in the United States. Douglass had introduced Harriet to William Seward, a Republican-party presidential hopeful who had opposed the Fugitive Slave Act. Seward loaned Harriet the money to purchase land for her home in Auburn, New York. Sarah Bradford, a writer, became impressed with the activities of Harriet and with Harriet's assistance wrote the book *Scenes in the Life of Harriet Tubman*. Through the sale of the book, Harriet was able to add to the loan from Seward to further finance her property, giving her family a home of their own.

As a person committed to abolishing slavery and ending injustices, as well as with her high profile in free society,

JOHN BROWN

A convention was called in Chatham to plan for the overthrow of slavery in the United States and the government that supported it. Headed by John Brown, a White abolitionist, sessions were held first at the British Methodist Episcopal Church on May 8, 1858 to create a Provisional Constitution for the United States. By his third meeting, Brown had attracted 35 Blacks and 11 Whites but his plans to make a surprise assault in the United States had been leaked, so he postponed his ill-fated raid on Harper's Ferry, Virginia, for a year. Brown was given the full support of the office of the Provincial Freeman and others supported Brown as well as they could. In Canada, Brown had supporters who were willing to return to the United States to lead an army of slave liberation , from St. Catharines, Ingersoll, Hamilton and North Buxton. The raid on Harper's Ferry failed and Brown was executed on December 2, 1859.

Harriet Tubman

Harriet also became dedicated to the women's rights movement. With Sojourner Truth and other feminists, she used her reputation and contacts to bring attention to women's right to vote and she was able to raise money for organizations that assisted women.

By 1860, Harriet had managed to free her entire family and she had completed 19 rescues freeing some 300 people. Harriet never lost a passenger and none of the people she freed was ever recaptured. Once she returned to live in the United States, she was drawn into the struggle between the northern Union forces and the Confederacy of the south, between those who wanted freedom for the slaves and the slave holders. During the Civil War, in the fall of 1862, she joined the Union forces at Hilton Head, South Carolina, and acted as a nurse, becoming acting head of the hospital. The only money she was given was $200, which she used to set up a washing house. She needed more money so she baked pies and made root beer in the evenings, selling these goods so she would have money to support herself. While she worked with the sick and wounded, she applied her own healing herbs and plants that she had seen used by her family and other slaves with great results.

By 1863 Harriet had gone from nursing to spy work and scouting for the Union forces. Harriet organized former slaves who had lived in areas of the South to assist in piloting rivers or identifying where food was stored. On a major raid on the Combahee River, near Charleston, South Carolina, Harriet is credited with being the person in charge of 300 Union troops and three gunboats which resulted in freedom for some 750 slaves. To this day, she continues to be the only American woman to lead a military action in American history.

Following the end of the American Civil War, Harriet did domestic work, partly out of necessity, as she was not given a military pension of her own. She used whatever money she got to support

FREDERICK DOUGLASS

He was born as a slave in 1817 near Easton, Maryland, but escaped from slavery in 1838 to Massachusetts. As a self-emancipated man, Douglass worked for the Anti-Slavery Society in New Bedford, Massachusetts which resulted in his travelling to Great Britain, where friends purchased his freedom from his master. His many speaking engagements on slavery while there earned him enough money to establish his own influential abolitionist newspaper, the North Star, in Rochester, New York, upon his return to the United States. He raised money in support of John Brown and his failed raid on Harper's Ferry and as a result fled to Canada. He later returned to the United States where he continued to speak on the need for Blacks to remain in the United States to help rebuild it, helped recruit Blacks for the Union Army, and fought for emancipation and the right to vote. After the Civil War, he became a Marshall for the District of Colombia, Recorder of Deeds and Counsel-General to Haiti. He died in Washington on February 20, 1895.

her extended family living with her and later to purchase an additional lot of land beside her home in Auburn. Harriet wanted to establish a shelter for Blacks, and the Harriet Tubman Home for Aged and Indigent Negroes was created. This site in Auburn and the British Methodist Episcopal Church in St. Catharines are now historical sites dedicated to this strong and selfless individual.

Harriet lived a long life and died at the age of 93. She was buried with military rites in Forest Hill Cemetery in Auburn, New York.

SOJOURNER TRUTH

Sojourner Truth (c.1797-1883) was born a slave in Hurley, New York, and lived to see most of her 13 children sold into slavery. She gained her emancipation in 1827. A tall, impressive woman, she became involved with abolitionists and was a staunch supporter of President Lincoln, whom she credits for freeing the slaves. Deeply religious, she took the name Sojourner Truth and gave numerous presentations on the need for the abolition of slavery, women's rights and temperance. She was an effective speaker who believed that she was called by God to deliver her messages. Her epitaph, "Is God Dead", was her response to the despair of some people at the lack of hope for Black people in the United States.

Harriet Tubman Home
180 South St.
Auburn, New York

MARY ANN CAMBERTON SHADD

The First Black Woman Publisher
Educator, Writer, Lecturer, Suffragette, Lawyer

BORN: October 9, 1823 Wilmington, Delaware
DEATH: June 5, 1893 Washington, DC.

MARY WAS BORN A "FREE" PERSON, the fourth generation of the Shadd family to be born free in a country that still had slave-holding states. With the passage of the Fugitive Slave Act in the United States in 1850, Mary, an experienced teacher, came to Windsor, Ontario, to educate the large number of refugees , both escaped slaves and "free persons", who had come to Canada from the United States. Mary began writing to advise those Blacks living in Canada and those considering escaping to Canada about the opportunities that existed in Canada. Mary established, wrote, edited and published a newspaper, the *Provincial Freeman*, to spread information about the anti-slavery movement, to state her claims of the wrongs of slavery and to highlight the achievements of the Blacks in Canada. She was the first Black woman publisher in North America and the editor of the first abolition paper in Canada. Later in her life she became a lawyer, the first Black woman to complete her law studies, and an advocate of equal rights for women, lecturing in the United States.

Harriet Shadd, mother

THE EARLY YEARS

Mary was the eldest of thirteen children born to Abraham and Harriet Parnell Shadd, and she was affectionately branded a rebel from an early age. Mary was aware that her family was involved in helping slaves who were seeking their freedom because her home, which housed her father's shoemaking business, was a station on the Underground Railroad. Her parents were so committed to ending slavery that they were willing to risk their freedom and their lives, as well as the lives of their children, to assist in any way they could to end slavery. From these beginnings, Mary was able to understand the problems of slavery and the challenges of freedom.

Abraham Shadd, father

Mary was influenced by the philosophy of her father, Abraham. He encouraged the free Blacks of Wilmington to improve themselves through education, and to save what little money they received for their labour and hard work. Abraham later became the President of the National Convention for the Improvement of Free People of Color and was opposed to the idea of free Blacks returning to Africa as he felt that Blacks should be able to receive an education, suitable housing and adequate career opportunities in the land of their birth — the United States. Equality was a goal that he felt should be the responsibility both of those with money and influence in society as well as those who were disadvantaged. To ensure an education for his children, Abraham moved the family to West Chester, Pennsylvania, a free state, as no schools existed for Black children in the slave state of Delaware.

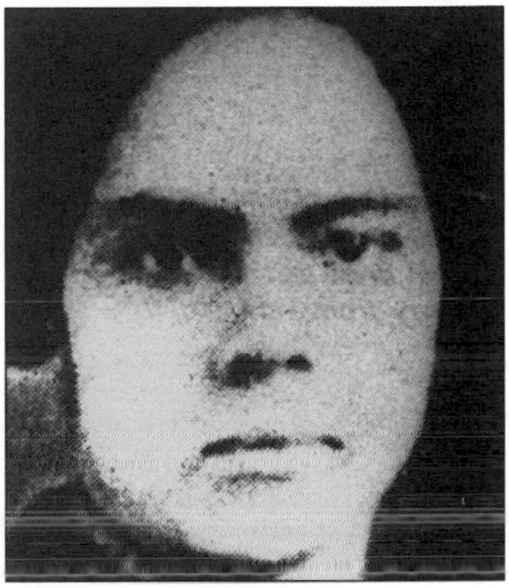

After only six years of schooling at a boarding school operated by Quakers, 16-year old Mary had had more education than most people and she was ready to teach others. She returned to Wilmington where she opened a school for Black children. Later, she also taught in West Chester, Pennsylvania, New York City and Norristown, Pennsylvania. In all her teaching she was praised for her abilities and dedication. Perhaps wishing to pass her vision on to others, she wrote a pamphlet, "Hints to the Colored People of the North" in 1849, encouraging Blacks to be thrifty and to follow a careful budget. This pamphlet was reviewed by both Martin Delaney, the first Black person to graduate from Harvard University, and Frederick Douglass, publicist of the *North Star* and leader in the anti-slavery movement. Both were impressed with the article she had written and found it a valuable document. Mary then began to write articles for the *North Star*, covering issues such as the right to vote for Blacks. While it was unusual for a woman to express herself publicly, Mary was passionate about improving the position of Blacks in America, and Mary was a spirited woman, not bound by the conventions of her gender or the stereotypes of her race.

Mary Ann Shadd

In 1850, The Fugitive Slave Act was passed in the United States. With this Act, all the legal power of the country was available to support the catching of slaves, anywhere in the United States. There was no freedom possible for freedom seekers or for people who had never known the bitter taste of the whip or the glare of the overseer.

SIMCOE AND ABOLITION

As a colony of Great Britain, the governing of Canada came under the responsibility of government administrators from Great Britain. The first Lieutenant-Governor of Upper Canada (now Ontario), John Graves Simcoe, had been a supporter of political reformer William Wilberforce in England, who was an abolitionist. After his appointment as Lieutenant Governor, Simcoe immediately announced that he would not "discriminate by dishonest policy between the Natives of Africa, America or Europe". In cooperation with Chief Justice William Osgoode and Attorney-General John White, a bill was drafted and introduced to the Legislative Assembly of Upper Canada to make a beginning to end slavery in 1793. Simcoe was moved to act because of a case where a Loyalist-owned slave, Chloe Cooley, was returned forcibly to slavery in the United States by virtue of being sold to an American. The opposition of slave-owning legislators to the bill reduced it to prohibiting the importation of slaves into Upper Canada. The new law also freed children born of slaves by their 25th birthday, making Upper Canada, now Ontario, the first British territory to legislate against slavery.

Slavery had been abolished in Canada since August 1, 1834. Upper Canada, now Ontario, had been one of the first governments to introduce anti-slavery legislation when, in 1793, Lieutenant-Governor Simcoe had brought in restrictions on importing slaves and the term a person could be enslaved, giving Upper Canada the appearance of being supportive of human dignity and equality for all people. The free Blacks, escaped slaves and Black Loyalists who were in Canada before 1850 were now joined by great numbers of Blacks from the United States seeking to achieve or maintain their liberty. Mary decided to join those in Canada, not from concern about her own well-being but because she anticipated a need for her teaching abilities for the growing Black population. She also wanted to determine the suitability of Canada as a secure haven for Blacks forced to consider moving from their homes because of the Fugitive Slave Act.

BLACK LOYALISTS

During the American War of Independence, the British military and government officials invited "rebel-owned" male slaves, and later any slave, to join their side. Blacks were promised the same grants of land for their military service and loyalty to the British Crown as non-Blacks, but these promises were not kept. At the end of the war and the movement of Loyalists to Canada, the Caribbean or Britain, any grant of land that a Black Loyalist did receive was often too small, too poor for farming or far too remote to be useful.

On her way to Windsor from a meeting in Toronto, Mary was convinced by Henry and Mary Bibb, the publishers of the newspaper, the *Voice of the Fugitive*, and administrators of the Refugee Home Society, to establish her school in Windsor because, they argued, it was in Windsor that the need was the greatest. There, Blacks were denied entry to public schools and had to start their own schools because of the Common Schools Act, which provided for separate schools for Blacks and Roman Catholics. However, Mary's strongly held views about integrated schools immediately brought her into conflict with the Bibbs, who were opposed to her operating an integrated school in an abandoned army building, known as "The Old Barracks". Teachers of Blacks had to use their own salaries to pay for supplies, fuel and at times building rentals, and, because Mary's school was a private

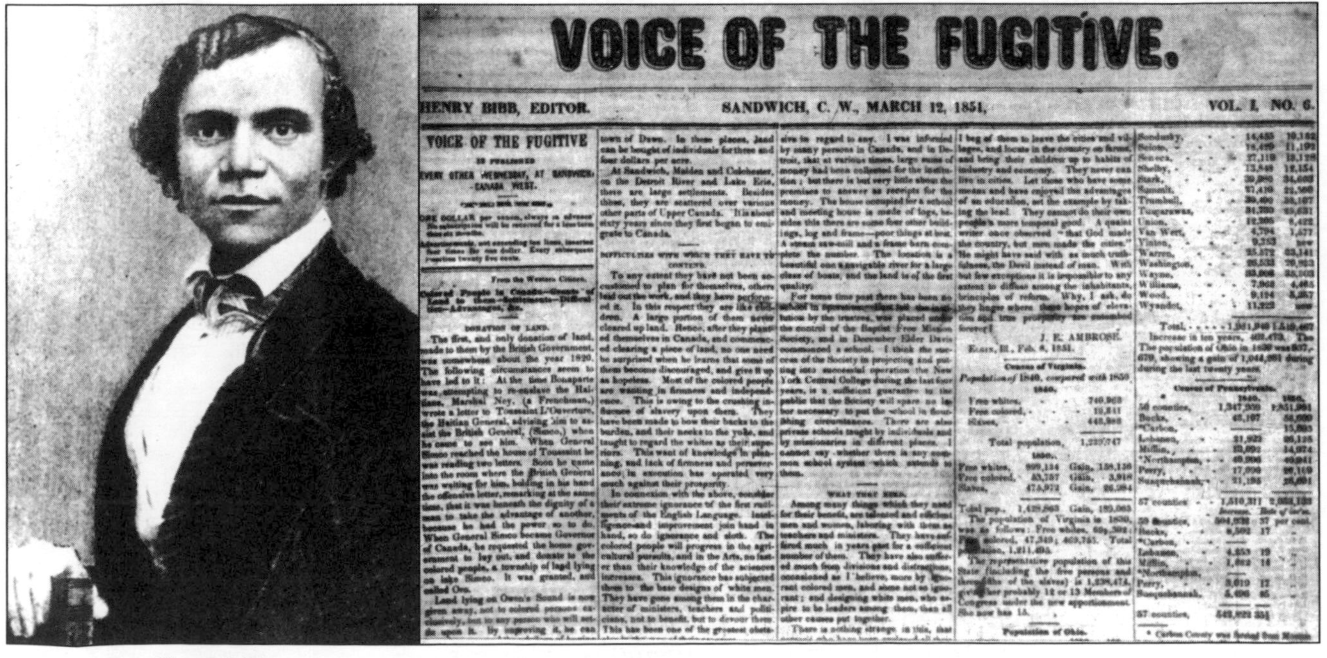

VOICE OF THE FUGITIVE.

HENRY BIBB, EDITOR. SANDWICH, C. W., MARCH 12, 1851. VOL. I. NO. 6.

VOICE OF THE FUGITIVE
IS PUBLISHED
EVERY OTHER WEDNESDAY, AT SANDWICH, CANADA WEST.

Henry Bibb

school, her salary was derived from her 20 students paying a tuition of 37 cents a month, which was beyond the ability of some families to pay.

Following advice from the Bibbs, who may have had the interests of the students at heart, Mary contacted George Whipple of the American Missionary Association, to obtain financial assistance. Through them, Mary was granted "half support" or half of the annual salary for a teacher. In accepting this donation, Mary became the only Black among the 263 teacher-missionaries funded by the AMA. In order to obtain the rest of her salary through school support, she still needed to have her students pay their fees. Mary was told that some parents might not pay once they found out she had received a grant. To prevent parents, who were able to pay, from withholding their tuition, Mary was advised to keep the receipt of the money to herself. The tuition plus the half-support gave Mary a salary of $250, which would have been the average annual salary for a Black person to receive at that time. However, by the summer of 1852, the Bibbs had made public in the *Voice of the Fugitive* the receipt of Mary's grant from the AMA and suggested that Mary was receiving a full-support grant before Mary had the opportunity to disclose the news herself. This conflict between Mary and the Bibbs caused an on-going hostility between them.

HENRY BIBB AND THE REFUGEE HOME SOCIETY

Born a slave in Kentucky in 1815, Bibb escaped to freedom by 1837, only to be recaptured while attempting to rescue his wife, Mary. Again seeking their freedom, the Bibbs made their way to Detroit where Henry became an effective anti-slavery speaker. With the passing of the Fugitive Slave Act in 1850 in the United States, the Bibbs moved to Windsor and founded the newspaper, the *Voice of the Fugitive*, for Blacks who had just escaped to Canada and to address issues of concern not covered by other newspapers.

The Refugee Home Society was established to provide assistance to Blacks who recently had escaped to freedom. With the support of the American Missionary Association and co-administered by White missionaries, Henry Bibb was responsible for not only providing land to freedom-seekers but also purchasing land which would remain under the control of the Refugee Home Society. These lands spread beyond the Windsor-Detroit area. His wife, Mary, operated a school for Blacks under the auspices of the Refugee Home Society.

While still teaching and waiting to find out about her support from the AMA, Mary researched, edited and published a booklet entitled "Notes On Canada West," which provided a detailed account of the positive aspects of life in present-day Ontario, including housing, employment, natural resources, churches and schools. Her booklet was so carefully written that she is credited with being the first Black woman to use information and statistics for propaganda purposes, of painting an appealing picture of Canada to counter the negative image that Canada had been given by slave owners in the United States trying to discourage the escaping slaves from going to Canada.

It became clear to Mary and others, that the Bibbs were not effectively assisting fugitives in Canada despite their public assertions that they were. Land, food , clothing and books donated to the Refugee Home Society, which was administered by the Bibbs, were not being given out to fugitives and Mary observed that the Bibbs were becoming wealthy owning land privately that was intended

Rev. Samuel Ward

REV. SAMUEL RINGGOLD WARD

When Ward was three years old, his enslaved parents escaped with him to New York City. Trained as a minister, Ward later worked among the Blacks who had escaped to Canada in Toronto and Chatham with the support of the Toronto Anti-Slavery Society. His strong abolitionist opinions made him an ally of Mary Ann Shadd and fostered the beginning of the *Provinicial Freeman*. He was identified as the editor of that paper as people would not accept Mary, a woman, as the editor of the newspaper.

for public use. Mary concluded that individual private donations as well as the significant financial backing of the AMA to the Refugee Home Society were being pocketed by the Bibbs, and other "begging agents," sometimes keeping for their own use as much as 60 percent of the money that they collected for the fugitives. To the outspoken and highly moral Mary, this was a situation that needed to be exposed and changed.

Mary began a letter-writing campaign to AMA officials to advise them of her concerns and she began to write articles for American anti-slavery newspapers to make them aware of the problems with the Refugee Home Society. The more unshakable Mary was in alerting others to the actions of the Society, the more she was attacked personally by the *Voice of the Fugitive*, which was, of course, controlled by Bibb. In August, 1852, Reverend Samuel Ward, who was a brilliant speaker, came to the Windsor area on a tour sponsored by the Anti-Slavery Society of Canada. He immediately became involved and wrote articles for Bibb's *Voice of the Fugitive*. Ward's views differed from Bibb's so this business relationship soon ended. Mary and Reverend Ward then joined forces as they held similar views and because Bibb, who was initially pleased to publish the writings of such a well-known person as Reverend Ward, soon became less interested in including passages which directly questioned his own ideas on dealing with the issue of racial separation.

Provincial Freeman.

DEVOTED TO ANTI-SLAVERY, TEMPERANCE, AND GENERAL LITERATURE.

VOLUME I.

JOSIAH HENSON AND THE DAWN SETTLEMENT

Josiah was a faithful slave who escaped from his owner only when he discovered that he was about to be sold. Henson escaped to Canada in 1830 and settled in an area near Dresden, Ontario. He established the Dawn Settlement there with funding from the American Missionary Association and private donations. The settlement was established to provide an organized Black community for fugitive slaves where they could live as free persons. In 1849, Henson had his autobiography published. While the settlement did not survive, his image as "Uncle Tom" from the novel *Uncle Tom's Cabin*, by Harriet Beecher Stowe, did survive because of the connection between himself and a character in the best-selling, anti-slavery book of the time. He died near Dresden, Ontario, on May 5, 1883.

By January 1853, the AMA suspended Mary because of her "peculiar religious convictions", although the real reasons may have been because she was outspoken and a woman. Mary was an intelligent, analytical and outspoken woman who did not readily defer to others. She did not fit the usual pattern of a woman of the time. As an independent thinker, she might have an unknown effect on her students and certainly the negative publicity her charges brought to the AMA and the Refugee Home Society did little to please them. It was easier for them to let Mary go rather than Henry Bibb. Mary continued to teach without their support until March 1853, and Bibb, feeling victorious, increased his personal attacks on Mary in his newspaper.

EDITOR AND PUBLISHER

Mary encouraged Ward to lend his name, as editor, to a new publication which would share their anti-slavery and integrationalist views to counter the claims of Bibb's newspaper. Because of the conventional thinking on the role of women, they decided to conceal the fact that Mary would be doing the real work of establishing, writing, editing and publishing. The first issue of the *Provincial Freeman* was launched in March 1853, as a response to the accidental death of a young Black male member of a debating society, a debating society that was operated by Mary Shadd and Reverend Ward, and which was being sensationalized in Bibb's newspaper.

Mary and Samuel were both committed to presenting the lifestyle, culture and activities of the free Black Canadian population in a positive manner and were clearly not going to allow their activities to be questioned in the public eye. The *Voice of the Fugitive* was read around the world and so the ideas expressed in it were read by people with different backgrounds and interests. Black publications tended to be read by educated and affluent Blacks as well as those interested in the question of abolition. It was felt that to permit the negative and often inaccurate comments of Bibb to go unchallenged would feed into those forces that maintained stereotypes about Blacks and saw freedom as an unsuitable solution for them. As individuals who had been able to gain an education and were able to express themselves intelligently, Mary and Ward were determined to fight racism with their words. The motto chosen for the *Provincial Freeman* was "Self Reliance is the True Road to Independence" and if they did not present an accurate account of the tragedy of the accidental death of the man, who would?

BACK TO AFRICA

At several different times, groups of Blacks in the Caribbean, the United States or Canada considered moving back to their ancestral homeland, Africa, because they did not have the range of rights and freedoms that non-Blacks had. Sometimes, emigration was encouraged by Whites as a way to get rid of people thought to be undesirable; sometimes emigration was encouraged as a source of Black pride by individuals such as Marcus Garvey; and sometimes emigration was viewed as the only viable option for people denied the land and assistance promised to them when they came to Canada as Black Loyalists.

With increasing financial debt, the departure of Ward on a speaking tour on abolition and the escalation of Bibb's attacks, Mary realized that she had to do some fundraising to support her newspaper. She travelled throughout the northern United States address-

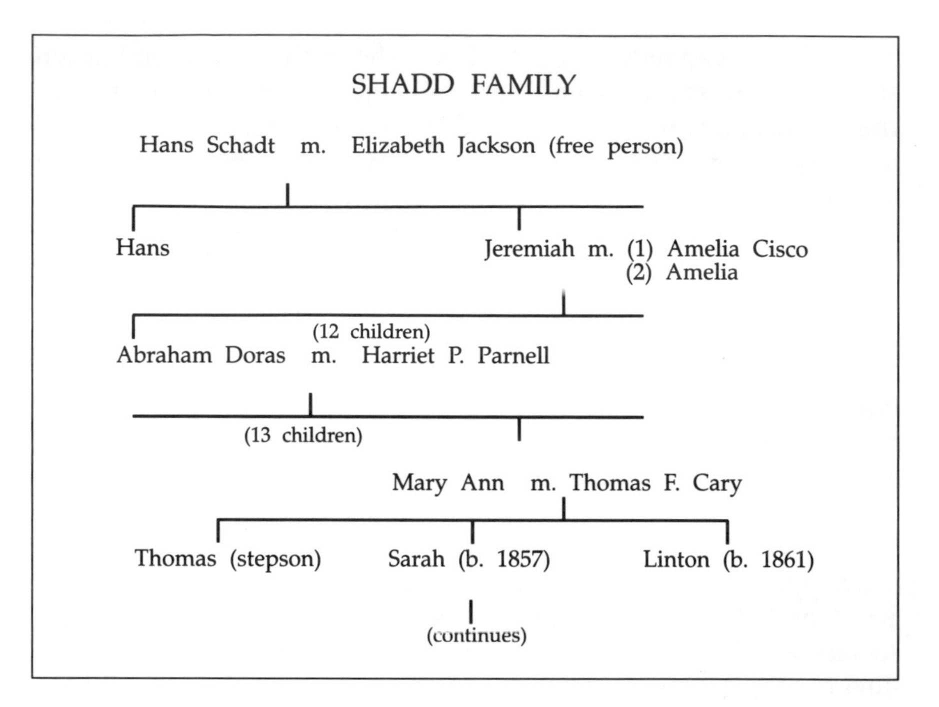

ing people and selling subscriptions to the newspaper until 1854 when she decided to set up her headquarters in Toronto, which was an anti-slavery haven, at least compared to many other places. The *Provincial Freeman* was now run from an office at 5 City Buildings, King Street East, with the notice that readers could contact "M.A.Shadd" with their letters and articles She signed her articles simply with a double asterisk (**) to hide her gender.

Controversy was soon to follow as Mary was infuriated to discover that abolitionists in Toronto were supporting a fundraising event for the Afro-American, Frederick Douglass, and they had not supported her. She wondered, in an editorial, if abolitionists were opposed to Black emigration from the United States since Douglass was strongly committed to Blacks remaining there and not coming to Canada. She wondered if they were supporting him because they really were not sure he would be successful in convincing Blacks to remain in the United States. A flood of replies expressing acceptance of Blacks in Canada came into the offices of the *Provincial Freeman* and the debate was carried within Canada as well as around the world.

THE SHADD FAMILY

Mary Ann Shadd is known for her writing and publishing but her brothers and sister were very accomplished as well. Emaline won the first prize for students at Toronto Normal School (Teachers' College) in 1855 for graduating first in her class. She began as a teacher in Kent and Peel Counties in Ontario before spending some time as an instructor at Howard University, in Washington, and then returned to Chatham, Ontario. Abraham Shadd served in the Union Army during the American Civil War. Alfred Shadd taught at the Buxton Mission School, while Garrison became a prosperous farmer near Chatham, Ontario. Isaac became involved with the *Provincial Freeman* and helped to publish it.

While investigating the activities of Josiah Henson and the Dawn Settlement near Dresden, Ontario, Mary met Thomas Cary and they formed part of a group of concerned Black citizens who were following the court case exploring the finances of the Dawn Settlement. Thomas Cary, a barber and owner of an ice house, had been an early supporter of the *Provincial Freeman*. The relationship between Mary and Thomas grew and on January 3, 1856, Mary married Thomas Cary and became stepmother of his child from a previous marriage. A little over a year later their first child was born on August 7, 1857. Neither marriage nor parenting stopped her activism, although she had waited several months before advising her readers that she had become married. She anticipated another outcry when they learned that "M.A.Shadd" was not only a woman but also a mother. In fact, public sentiment was so strong in reaction to the news that she was a woman that Mary and Thomas decided to move to Chatham to get away from the protests against her.

In 1858 the staff of the *Provincial Freeman* drew straws to determine who would go to the United States to report on the status of John Brown's plans and Osborne Anderson was the person selected to go. Brown thought that slavery could be overthrown by freeing and then training slaves to fight. His unsuccessful raid on Harper's Ferry, West Virginia, was reported by Anderson, who was the only Black Canadian to be involved and witness the raid as well as one of the only people to escape from the raid. Mary edited Anderson's account and published it as "A Voice from Harper's Ferry".

Mary's husband, Thomas Cary, died on November 29, 1860, before Mary gave birth to their second child in the spring of 1861. Mary continued to publish the *Provincial Freeman* with her brother, Isaac, when they could raise sufficient funds to publish. Money from subscriptions or speaking engagements helped to fund the paper, as did the printing services they provided to the City of Chatham. Sometimes, however, this was not enough to support her family and buy supplies to print another edition of the paper. She also supported herself and her family by writing articles for other newspapers until the start of the Civil War in the United States. When Mary was asked by Martin Delaney to recruit Blacks for the Union side of the conflict, she became the only paid Black woman recruitment agent in the United States. During the Civil War, in 1863, the Proclamation of Emancipation was passed in the United States abolishing slavery and when the Civil War came to an end in 1865, Blacks, who had escaped to Canada, began to return to the United States. This was partly because of the pull of freedom in the land of their birth and partly because of the changing tolerance towards non-Whites here. Mary too returned to the United States and obtained her teaching certificate in Detroit in 1868 and moved her family to Washington, D.C. a year later to continue to be where she felt she was most needed.

Isaac D. Shadd

Mary taught and was principal of three schools during the day and at night she attended the Law School of Howard University in

Washington. She was the first Black woman to attend law school and complete her program. She completed her studies in 1872 but was not allowed to graduate because she was a woman, and one with a high profile. It was not until 1881 that she was given her degree. As a 58-year old lawyer, Mary sometimes provided her services without charge because of her concern for underprivileged people. To support her family, Mary earned money during the summers by selling subscriptions for "Era", a publication of Frederick Douglass; by writing articles for "Era" and for John Wesley Cromwell's paper, the *Advocate*, and through selling copies of William Still's book, *The Underground Railroad*. Her commitment to hard work and self-sufficiency is evident.

I would rather wear out than rust out.

Mary died on June 5, 1893 in Washington, D.C. and is buried there in Harmony Cemetery.

Mary Ann Camberton Shadd held strong beliefs about the means by which Black people could improve their condition once they were released from bondage. Like her father, she strongly advocated education, hard work and thrift as the means of developing self-respect and achieving integration as equals into mainstream society. She followed her own advice and became the first Black woman publisher in North America, one of the first woman editors of an anti-slavery paper in Canada and the first Black salaried recruitment agent in the United States. Also, she left a living legacy as many Blacks living in Toronto, Windsor, Amherstburg, North Buxton and Chatham , as well as Afro-Americans in Washington, D.C., and New Orleans, where a branch of the family later moved, can trace their ancestry back to this forceful woman. Through her dedication, determination and commitment to improve the position of all people, particularly the disadvantaged, she made a significant difference to life in North America.

THE BLACK PRESS

The main purpose of the Black press in Canada was to provide information about the Black community to the reader and to provide a mechanism for responding to the reporting found in the non-Black press. This was necessary as reporting in the non-Black press was not always accurate or positive regarding the events in the African-Canadian community. As some of the Black population were illiterate or had limited reading skills because of the restrictions on slaves and limited political power , Black papers had a readership from both the Afro-Canadian community, who could read, and the rest of the society.

The *Voice of the Fugitive* and the *Provincial Freeman* were two of the first Black newspapers in Canada. The *Voice of the Fugitive* included detailed articles and was started before the *Provincial Freeman* was launched on March 25, 1853. The biting, analytical style of the *Provincial Freeman* included descriptions of abolitionist activities. Growing discontent with the issue of slavery and grievances about settlement were common themes for people who wished to have improvements in society and were evidenced by both papers. Freedom-seekers were encouraged to participate in their communities and to be good citizens.

CARRIE BEST

Poet, Journalist, Writer, Broadcaster, Civil Rights Worker, Humanitarian and Community Advocate

BORN: March 4, 1903 New Glasgow, Nova Scotia

CARRIE BECAME DEEPLY INVOLVED IN THE AFFAIRS OF HER COMMUNITY and the rights of its members when she was a young wife and mother. She founded the *Clarion*, a newspaper with nation-wide circulation, as a forum to express her observations and concerns. To contribute to the history of Nova Scotia, she has written a personal biography, which includes details about Maritime life as it has affected all underprivileged residents of the province. And, to share her love of poetry, she has produced and narrated a radio program "The Quiet Corner", which was broadcast on five radio stations in the province of Nova Scotia. Carrie has been appointed to the Order of Canada, first as a Member, then as an Officer, in recognition of her humanitarian activities.

LITTLE TRACADIE

This Black settlement at the northern end of Nova Scotia, in what is now Guysborough County, was created as a way to give land to a group of Black Loyalists. Each of the 74 Black Loyalist families was given a farm of 40 acres (16 hectares) for their service to the Crown; still others received such small plots that were impossible to cultivate. Other Black settlements were also created for groups of Black Loyalists, the largest was Birchtown, near Shelburne, which had the largest population of free people of African descent outside Africa with 1,500 people in the mid 1800s.

THE EARLY YEARS

Carrie is the fourth generation of her family to be born and raised in Little Tracadie, Guysborough County, near New Glasgow, Nova Scotia. Her parents both worked to support their family. She was the middle child, with two brothers and she describes the family as "poor but respectable". Even as a little girl, Carrie knew that she would be exploring new directions from those around her and that it would be more difficult because

Dr. Best received her Doctor of Laws degree in 1975.

she was Black. She found that the lack of a positive image of Blacks in Canada made it more difficult to form her own identity, but it was not impossible.

Carrie's father was a labourer with a small trucking business. Her mother, who lacked a formal education, did have common sense on her side and maintained high standards in her home. She would tell her children, "Society has said you are an inferior being, born to be a hewer of wood and a drawer of water because you are Black. Remember you are a person, separate and apart from all other persons on earth. The path to your destiny is hidden: you alone must find it." Then, her mother would add, "Take the first right turn and go straight ahead!" The other great influence on her early learning was the poet Paul Lawrence Dunbar whose poetry was particularly meaningful to Carrie. Like her mother, Carrie had a fantastic ability to memorize immediately any speech or poem and Carrie seems to have started to build her personal file of such writing early in her life.

PAUL LAWRENCE DUNBAR

Dunbar was one of the earliest Black American writers and tended to produce poetry following the dialect and forms of speech used by African-Americans. His book of poetry, called *Little Brown Baby*, published in 1895, while not permitted to be used in schools because of the limits placed on the education of Blacks, was available outside the classroom where Dunbar's writing gained immense popularity.

Carrie's mother was such a good cook that she was often asked to cater for social functions in the town. At that time, Black women were not allowed to do anything except domestic work, such as housekeeping, babysitting and cooking, and there were social and institutional barriers to discourage or prevent non-Whites from other types of work. However, as Carrie has said," I was well trained in the housekeeping arts by my mother. I had decided very early that this type of work would be done for myself alone, and never as a means of livelihood." How could a Black woman who had graduated from high school in the 1920s think of doing something different?

HIGHER EDUCATION

Because there were larger numbers of Blacks who were affluent enough to contribute to the development of their own schools and because Blacks were usually not permitted to attend mainstream schools, Black colleges emerged in the United States. For many Blacks in Canada interested in a higher education, their only option was to go to these American colleges to obtain the skills they needed for white-collar jobs because they were routinely excluded from regular schools in Canada. It was expensive for a family to send their child away to school, so not every bright student had a chance to learn the skills they needed to move into higher paying positions and professions.

Initially, Carrie was accepted in a nursing program at Provident Hospital and Training School for Nurses in Chicago. As she became more confident, she discussed her plans for her career and was advised that she would be expelled if she fainted more than three times. Carrie realized that she might not be suited to nursing and she considered a career in teaching. She set out for her teaching post at Delaps Cove, Nova Scotia, ready to begin in January. On her way, she stayed with Addie Ruggles, a Black baker, and her family overnight. When Addie finished describing the isolation and small size of the town of Delaps Cove, the settlement where her sister lived with five other families, Carrie knew that she would not be able to live there and her career as a teacher ended that morning.

In 1925, Carrie married Albert Best, a railway porter with the Canadian National Railway, and a veteran of the First World War. They had a son, Calbert, and later adopted two girls, Sharyn and Berma, and with her husband away from home a great deal because of his job she was kept busy. With her husband Albert, Carrie became very involved in the community of New Glasgow and human rights issues. She had always loved to write and she gave poetry readings to help raise money for other Blacks in the community to help them pay their taxes. Later, her warmly written notes to her son and daughters, when they were in university, led to her writing letters to the editor.

A VOICE FOR THE COMMUNITY

Issues involving human rights and civil liberties compelled Carrie to develop stories and reports that allowed her thoughts and interpretations to be clearly and completely stated so that she could alert the public to events that were taking place perhaps without general knowledge. By 1946, Carrie founded the *Clarion* with her son, Calbert, to be the voice of "coloured Nova Scotians for promoting inter-racial understanding and goodwill". The *Clarion* was the first Black newspaper in Nova Scotia, making Carrie the first Black publisher in Nova Scotia. Carrie travelled throughout Nova Scotia, basing her articles on her own investigations of the degree of discrimination she found in restaurants, hotels, theatres and other public places. Blacks were not served or not served in turn or not admitted to certain establishments, so Carrie visited them herself to see how she would be treated, then wrote about it so everyone would know. The year 1946 was the year when the terrible treatment of Viola Desmond, Canada's Rosa Parks, agitated civil rights activists in Canada and the United States because Viola was imprisoned overnight for having sat in a "Whites Only" section of a theatre in Nova Scotia.

WORK OPPORTUNITIES

Many Blacks were interested in various types of jobs but they were often excluded. An employer might ask his staff to help him to find a new worker, so the job would not be advertised. Specialized training might be needed, but it was often difficult to enrol in courses for the necessary training. As well, libraries were often off limits to Black people. As a consequence, many Blacks were stuck in housekeeping and general labour jobs which paid very little and served to keep them powerless to make changes in their living conditions. High prestige jobs within the Black community tended to be connected to the church and the school, which were often segregated.

Clearly, major mainstream events were reported, but it was often the more personal stories that would touch Carrie the most and cause her to explore their impact on society. Carrie wrote about the body of a Black baby which was refused burial in the "White" cemetery of St. Croix, near Windsor, Nova Scotia, because of a by-law that had been passed in 1907 which stated that "No Negro, Indian or poor Coloured Person" was to be buried there. The story reached news media across Canada and the United States, resulting in Stockley Carmichael, a Black activist in the United States, and other Canadian and American civil rights leaders converging on Nova Scotia, to force changes that would not permit this to continue. This pressured the government of Nova Scotia to begin to examine unfair practices in the province that might exist against minority groups.

VIOLA DESMOND AND ROSA PARKS

Viola Desmond is the "Rosa Parks" of Canada. While in an area of Nova Scotia that was unfamiliar to her, she attended a show, sitting in the section locally known to be for "Whites Only". She was sent to jail and fined but her treatment and the objections to the segregation of the community caused an international uproar that resulted in the people of African descent in Nova Scotia organizing to fight for their rights as equal citizens.

On December 5, 1955 in Montgomery, Alabama, Rosa Parks, a Black woman, sat in a seat at the front of the bus, instead of the rear where Blacks were expected to sit. Her action sparked a year-long boycott by African-Americans of the public transportation system there. Ensuing events resulted in racial reform in the United States led by many, including the leadership given by Martin Luther King.

Through the *Clarion*, Carrie took on many different issues and concerns. Early in her career she had interest in issues on the environment and she fought against the prospect of attempts to interfere with tides of the Bay of Fundy. Carrie was also responsible for bringing attention to the unfair treatment given to the survivors and rescuers of the Springhill Mine disaster in Springhill, Nova Scotia.. A major mine cave-in at a large coal mine in Springhill had resulted in the death of many miners. But the treatment of survivors and rescuers was not the same for Whites and Blacks. Only White miners and rescuers were formally recognized. Carrie brought this to the attention of the public and the situation was quickly corrected so that all survivors of the disaster and rescuers were treated the same when her story reached the national press. Carrie decided to begin a nationwide circulation of the *Clarion* because she became interested in promoting a "national association for the advancement of coloured people", as existed in the United States, to focus attention on the experience, activity and vitality of Blacks in Canada.

Carrie Best.

The *Clarion* ceased publication in 1956 but Carrie remained active with human rights activities, writing for the *Nova Scotia Gleaner* and the Halifax *Herald*. At a speaking engagement, Carrie's ability to help people understand complex, unfair or hurtful issues so impressed George Cadogan, editor of the Pictou *Advocate* that he invited Carrie to write a regular column for that newspaper. Usually, at that time, the only way Blacks could get their names in the newspaper was when they were identified by name and colour in a reported crime. Through her investigative reporting, she was able to change this so that there was more balanced coverage of the activities of Blacks. Carrie continued reporting for the newspaper from 1968 to 1975 and made significant contributions for her general reporting and her investigative reporting.

In one incident, labelled the "Vale Road Saga" by Carrie, she reported the sale of a lakefront property that belonged to a newly widowed, 59-year old, illiterate Black woman, to a 25-year old White man who was the principal of a rural school. The sale took place in an Antigonish grocery store and the grieving woman, who was vulnerable because of the recent death of her husband and because she could not read, did not have legal or professional advice. Since her land and home of 25 years was assessed at $15,000 and the price paid by the purchaser was only $2500 it appeared that a most unfair deal had been arranged and that they had taken advantage of the emotionally distraught woman. Carrie investigated this unjust deal and brought it to the attention of the public through her articles in the newspaper.

The "Vale Road Saga" stretched on for over six years and was a long and costly battle for Carrie, who thereafter continued to be amazed at her level of involvement when it seemed so unrealistic to expect a change in the outcome of this case, because of experiences in similar cases in the province in the past. It was only by chance that Carrie became aware that there was something worth investigating. In 1968, she was reading a list of properties in which taxes had not been paid, and all were owned by Blacks in one neighbourhood. This was curious as the town was sufficiently large to have persons from other areas and other ethnic groups not paying their taxes. Carrie felt that this small pocket of homes was being targetted because areas of industrial and commercial development planned for the area. Instead of being able to offer a fair price for their homes, these people were to be pressured or forced out of them as the plans for the development were put into effect. When Carrie began to ask probing questions about this issue at the local registry offices, she found herself having to choose between paying a fine or spending one hour in jail for a traffic violation, which she suspected was created to obstruct her further investigation. The experience made Carrie more determined to uncover all that she could since she felt that if it was so crucial to silence her with municipal force then there must indeed be a story waiting for her to uncover.

As she continued to uncover other issues in the Pictou *Advocate*, Carrie also published her weekly findings and speculations about the Vale Road developments in an exhausting series of articles and columns. The memory of the Black residents of Africville being moved in garbage trucks by the city of Halifax after the city took over their property and bulldozed their church in the name of

AFRICVILLE

Both the Black Loyalists, who had been promised land grants but instead got little or nothing, and escaped slaves found themselves in need of homes. Some of these people were forced to use whatever land they could find and build homes and their churches with whatever they could salvage. They assumed ownership of some land near Halifax so that they were close enough to the city to find service jobs,and yet far enough away to avoid the constant racism directed at them. A warm, supportive, interdependent community developed that lasted for generations until the City of Halifax relocated the community and bulldozed their homes in the name of urban renewal. The area is now a park and a monument marks the sight of the Seaview Baptist Church, which was the social centre of the community.

urban renewal was still strong, and Carrie did not want to see this happen to the residents of Vale Road, in the guise of the need for industrial expansion. She saw these residents as victims, their homes being classified as inadequate, although 20 years before these same people had been denied the opportunity to participate in a co-operative housing scheme that would have allowed them to have homes they could afford and maintain.

As an advocate for the residents of the Vale Road area, Carrie , at the request of the Premier of Nova Scotia, brought her collection of research to the attention of the Director of Human Rights Commission to support her charges that the Town of New Glasgow had "abused its tax powers in an effort to obtain the land of poor people." This led to further investigations by officials.

Most of the suffering of most people,
no matter what race or creed,
is ignorance of the economic environment in which
most people find themselves.

A report prepared for the Human Rights Commission, the Boyd Report, showed that large land plots owned by businessmen had low assessment rates and the small land areas owned by the poor people had been given high assessment rates. This meant that poor people, whose property was often a humble dwelling in need of repair, were required to pay much more for their property taxes than the businessmen. As a result, some were forced to lose their property because they were unable to make their tax payment.

Carrie's love of poetry and her high profile in the community allowed her to produce and narrate her own radio program for over 12 years on five different radio stations. The show, called "The Quiet Corner", made Carrie a well-known personality as she recited or read passages from novels or poems to soothe or stimulate her listeners. Her commitment to expressing herself and to providing thoughtful versions of events allowed her to receive a grant from the province and the Canada Council to research Black history in Nova Scotia. She later printed her autobiography entitled *That Lonesome Road* through her own publishing company. She was the first to be awarded the Lloyd McInnes Memorial Award in 1970 for her contributions to public betterment and she received the first annual award by the National Black Coalition of Canada and an award from the African United Baptist Association.

Shortly after the death of her husband, Albert, Carrie decided to donate over five hectares of her property, in the city of Pictou, to the province for the creation of a park in the name of her husband. A grant helped to prepare the land for its planned use as a safe place for both seniors and children to visit and the park, named the Albert

The author, Rosemary Sadlier, and Carrie Best.

T. Best Park, was officially opened on August 21, 1972. In 1975, on the occasion of the 100th anniversary of the founding of the city of New Glasgow, it was decided to honour one Black resident to represent the Black community. However, Carrie was furious when she learned that the city had chosen a man who used to clean toilets, rather than a Black person who had made a significant contribution to the city. She knew there were many other Blacks who had made a contribution to the city and who were deserving of the award. Carrie initiated the decision to honour Reverend Donald Thomas. He had walked or borrowed cars in order to work in the community for over 30 years and was deserving for his leadership in the community. She felt he merited a car of his own. Carrie was able to raise enough money to purchase and present Reverend Donald Thomas with a new car at a huge affair as a tribute to him for his 30 years of service to the Black community.

On December 18, 1974, Carrie had been appointed a Member of the Order of Canada for her service to Canada and on December 17, 1979, Dr. Carrie Best was elevated to Officer of the Order of Canada. On May 11, 1975, she received the honorary degree of Doctor of Laws from St. Francis Xavier University at Antigonish, Nova Scotia. These prestigious awards, presented by the Governor General of Canada, indicate the impact that Carrie has made on the local and national consciousness.

When Kay Livingstone visited Nova Scotia to promote the formation of a Visible Minority Women's Society of Canada, Carrie and Kay became good friends and staunch mutual supporters. Unfortunately, Kay's death came shortly after and Carrie went on to become the founder and provincial coordinator of the Kay Livingstone Visible Minority Women's Society of Nova Scotia, which continued

KAY LIVINGSTONE

Born in London, Ontario, Kay Livingstone was an outstanding community worker and actress who was instrumental in starting a national organization of women of colour in Canada, known as the Visible Minority Women's Society.

their dream of women experiencing mutual support and respect for their talents and contributions to society.

In 1991, Carrie received yet another honour: an award for her outstanding contributions to human rights. Fittingly, it was received on the anniversary of the day the United Nations ratified the Declaration of Human Rights. As a leader in human rights and having achieved broad recognition, Carrie in her later years might have withdrawn to her home and family. But Carrie had more work to do and felt compelled to restart the *Clarion*. The first issue of the renewed *Clarion* was published in 1992 as a means of informing her readers, the court of public opinion, so that they can begin to examine the evidence put before them concerning issues.

The first issue of the renewed *Clarion* focused on a land-ownership dispute involving herself. It is sadly ironic that the issue relates to Carrie herself since she has spent much of her life helping to confront injustices for others. The land in question is in Pictou County, Nova Scotia, and the issues relate to the boundaries and the actual ownership of the property. Carrie hopes to live to see an agreeable solution as it is her wish to have something to leave for those she calls "the talented tenth", the one person out of ten who is gifted and is able to provide leadership, as the sale of the property would generate enough money to establish a trust fund for talented young people.

Dr. Carrie Best has made a difference because she helped to put the needs and concerns, the trials and triumphs, of all peoples in the open where the issues could best be identified or reformed. Her determination to see a problem through to the end, no matter how long it might take, has helped many who did not have the resources, the ability or the skill to do it for themselves. She is a fighter who is guided by her values and a "soul force" that keeps her going.

ROSEMARY BROWN

Social Worker, Politician, Writer, Social Activist

Born: June 17, 1930 Kingston, Jamaica

ROSEMARY CAME TO CANADA TO FURTHER HER EDUCATION after already learning about the importance of politics and political decisions during her childhood in Jamaica. Initially, Rosemary avoided participation in politics of any nature in Canada, but after completing her university degree, her marriage and motherhood, she was drawn into the peace movement and feminism. Rosemary was the first Black women elected to a provincial legislature, serving as a Member of the Legislative Assembly of British Columbia. She was also the first woman to seek the leadership of a federal political party., Her dedication to human rights has led her to the position of Head of the Ontario Human Rights Commission.

THE EARLY YEARS

Rosemary was the second of the three children of Ralph and Enid Wedderburn. With the untimely death of their father when Rosemary was only three-years old, Rosemary and the other children were left in the care of the family of Rosemary's mother. Through

Rosemary Brown

her early years, the constant care-giving roles were filled by Rosemary's grandmother, Imogine Wilson-James, her aunts, Leila James-Tomlinson and Gwen Shakleford and her uncle, Dr. Karl James. Rosemary was significantly influenced by these members of her family. Her grandmother believed in sharing with those who did not have much. Aunt Gwen went to West Africa with her husband to open a successful business and she was responsible for raising Rosemary's awareness of African culture; later, Gwen would pay for Rosemary's university education. Her uncle Karl was perhaps the person who most encouraged Rosemary to excel. He was a holder of an Order of the British Empire for his outstanding contribution to medicine, having helped to found the Cancer Institute of Jamaica.

It was her Aunt Leila, called Aunt Lil, however, who was Rosemary's most powerful role model. She was the first Jamaican woman to win a scholarship to the University of London and developed a comprehensive welfare system upon her return to Jamaica. Aunt Lil would later be appointed a Lay Judge and received a Member of the British Empire award. During the summers, Aunt Lil would take Rosemary with her across Jamaica in her travels to help disadvantaged people. Through these travels, Rosemary observed that despite hard work, many people continued to be poor because they had no control over the political and social policies that affected their lives. Aunt Lil encouraged Rosemary to always seek to know why a situation is the way it is, since one is in a better position to make changes and improve society by understanding the problems and issues.

At home, political issues were always being discussed and the issues of the day were explained to the Wedderburn children until they understood them. As a result, in addition to the strong women in her home, all of Rosemary's role models were politicians. Rosemary loved debating and often practised delivering speeches, imagining that she was a successful courtroom lawyer able to win cases on the sheer strength of her words and presentation. Her confidence in forming complicated ideas into convincing arguments is a skill that Rosemary has not lost.

Growing up in a home run by women, Rosemary saw women making decisions and working together. Because of this, environment, she was not intimidated by men. As a result, she tended to treat men and women alike as equals, whereas some women with backgrounds different to Rosemary's might have treated men with deference.

After reviewing the possibilities for higher education, it was decided that Rosemary should attend McGill University in Montreal. Canada had the reputation of being racially tolerant, unlike the traditional choice of Britain, and Rosemary was too vocal in her dislike of British policies regarding Jamaica. Her guardians thought

BEING A MINORITY

In many countries, people of colour form the majority of the population and it is their culture, music, philosophy, and other cultural influences, that are widely known. In Canada, when Rosemary Brown arrived, the "majority culture", of which Rosemary had been a part in Jamaica, no longer reflected or accepted her.

On a world basis, only 15% of the population is White while 85% of the world population is made up of people of colour. Being a minority does not mean belonging to a group having only a few members, it means belonging to a group that does not have control of what is mainstream, that does not have the power to broadly define and express culture, education and lifestyle issues.

that it would help to postpone her serious relationship with her steady boyfriend until she completed her university studies if she went to McGill University. At McGill, Rosemary was in a "minority" position and she felt unable to assume the privileges of a majority person, especially in dealing with immigration officers, in finding summer accommodation and later in trying to get a summer job to support herself during the school year. She blamed racism and it was frustrating and humiliating for her. She felt that her lack of experience with prejudice made it difficult for her to cope, even though there were others who had similar experiences. It was the warden in her residence who found Rosemary a summer job, but without her assistance Rosemary doubts that she would have been able to find one.

In the early 1950s, the influence of the right-wing elements, such as the influence of Senator McCarthy in the United States, had serious impact on minority groups in both countries. In Montreal, some politically active students from the West Indies were deported because officials were afraid of the changes they might make in people's thinking, making Rosemary feel a need to be careful in what she said and with whom she associated. She did remain socially active and, in fact, had three marriage proposals by her final year in university. In fact, she even went so far as to apply to different universities for different programs to match whichever of her suitor's career plans she would fit into. In a way, this was not uncommon in those days. She later would say, "Thinking back on it, I am appalled that all the life options that I considered on graduation revolved around my relationships with the men in my life." She is, therefore, pleased that students today are planning their lives according to their own goals and aspirations, quite independent of the direction of others.

MCCARTHYISM

During the early 1950s, there was a growing concern about the "Red Menace", the potential for the growth of communism in the United States and in the world. Communists were portrayed, especially by Senator Joseph McCarthy, as a threat to the survival of the United States and so a careful examination of leaders, thinkers and artists was begun to weed out all anti-American communist sympathizers. Many people who were concerned about the welfare of others were branded as communist and subsequently they were avoided, found that they could not be hired and even were imprisoned. Some were closely monitored by the CIA and files kept on their activities.

In Canada, the communist threat was also considered a reality. Students who were too far to the left politically were good targets for the government of the time, and if they were on visas, it was easy to send them back to their home countries, rather than having to deal with their assumed negative impact on society.

Hang on until one caring person in any given situation is found.

On August 12, 1955, Rosemary and Bill Brown were married in a small civil ceremony in Vancouver. Bill, who was born in Georgia, was completing his first year of medical school and in deciding to marry him, Rosemary knew that she might not return to Jamaica. Initially, Vancouver seemed to be more tolerant of visible minorities, but Rosemary soon found that it was difficult to find either a job or a place to live, even though plenty of both were available at that time. Finally, she did find a job and a place to live which led her to develop her "one person" philosophy: "to hang on until one person in any given situation is found". The one person who does not judge you by the colour of your skin and is sensitive to your

IMMIGRATION

All countries have systems for handling people who would like to immigrate or move within their boundaries. For a very long time, Canada gave preferential treatment to the applications of people from European countries. It was not until the 1960s that the immigration process began to encourage the immigration of non-European peoples and the establishment of more embassies worldwide.

individuality, the one person who is strong enough not to be bound by convention.

By 1957, the Browns had settled into a comfortable life with friends reflecting both backgrounds: Caribbean and North American. In 1957, their daughter, Cleta, was born and their son, Gary, was born in 1959. With their new role as parents, they realized that they should do what they could to make it a better world for their children. They were willing to take risks to safeguard the future of their children. They began to lobby for what they felt was right, sign petitions against what they thought was wrong and participate in peace marches. When Bill's parents died, his ties with the United States were severed and the Browns decided to become Canadian citizens. By this time, Rosemary was active politically and she soon found herself being encouraged to work as a social worker because of her concern for others.

Rosemary's experiences with her Aunt Lil had given her a grounding in how to help people help themselves. She had support from her family, which gave her strength, but she was not prepared for the human suffering that she encountered working with the Children's Aid Society. Having seen some of the poorer conditions of life, she was convinced that every child should be a wanted child. She wanted to continue with her work, but the family had to return to Montreal so that Bill could complete his medical program. There she worked with the Montreal Children's Hospital and was responsible for children who were accidentally brain damaged mainly through car accidents and not wearing seat belts. After this, she became a strong supporter of compulsory seat belt use.

After Bill completed his medical studies, they returned to Vancouver in 1964. Soon after returning Rosemary was shocked to have a pregnancy end with a stillbirth and she credits the support and feeling of sisterhood she developed with the women in her neighbourhood as helping her through this tragedy. She needed to become involved in some way and was offered a one-day-a-week televised social work position on a show called "People in Conflict". She gladly accepted and enjoyed doing that show, which also allowed her the time to complete her Master of Social Work degree before the birth of another son, Jonathon, in 1965.

The 1960s was a time of significant change as both the Black Power Movement and the Women's Movement challenged and changed racial and gender issues. As both a Black person and a woman, Rosemary did not feel that she could remove herself from either struggle, and she became active in both causes. At a conference to discuss the recommendations of the Royal Commission on the Status of Women, Rosemary represented the British Columbia Council of Black Women, the National Black Coalition of Canada, as the western representative, and Simon Fraser University, as she was active in these groups and it would save some expenses if she could

BLACK POWER

During the 1960s and 1970s, a number of racially motivated incidents against people of African descent, often costing innocent people their lives, forced African-Americans to challenge their treatment and demand changes. Within the Black community, re-education or consciousness raising resulted in the wearing of African clothing and the adoption of African-inspired hairstyles as a means of expressing and defining themselves as they sought to obtain greater political power and recognition. More militant members advocated more violent means to end the unfair treatment of Blacks.

go. She was appointed to develop an advocacy service for women similar to the Ombudsman, and she noted a distinct relationship between the problem of women's poverty and their dependent status in marriage. As well, there were inequities in the difference in wages between men and women, which was not acceptable in a society where men and women were supposed to be working equally. Rosemary's efforts on behalf of women, in particular the opposition of the amendment to an Act regarding the financial maintenance of wives' and children at a legislative Committee, brought her an invitation to run as a candidate for the New Democratic Party (NDP) for British Columbia.

Initially, Rosemary did not think that she could win an election since she was Black, female and an immigrant to Canada. However, she did see it as a once in-a-lifetime opportunity and running would give her the opportunity to highlight the goals of the community and the Royal Commission on the Status of Women so that feminist issues might receive national attention. The specific needs of women could be discussed so that everyone would not only understand but also help to change them. With the endorsement of the Vancouver Status of Women Council, Rosemary helped to form the government after the New Democratic Party won the provincial election. She was elected and represented the Vancouver Burrard riding in a day that she calls "her miracle". In that election, both she and Emery Barnes became the first people of African descent to win an election in British Columbia since the election of Mifflin Wistar Gibbs in Victoria in 1858.

Rosemary identifies her feminism as the most important influence in her life and politics. At the time of her election, the impact of the feminist movement was being felt inside the government as the NDP government became the first government to fund rape crisis centres, transition houses and women's health collectives in Canada. During the period when the NDP was the government of British Columbia and Rosemary was an elected representative, child care spaces rose dramatically from 2,500 to 18,603 by 1975 and a woman was chosen head of the Human Rights Commission to support further the new human rights code, which prohibited discrimination on the basis of sex or marital status.

WOMEN'S MOVEMENT

The women's movement was born of the discontent women felt with their treatment and their power in society. Women, like many other minority groups, knew that they were being paid less for the same work and that promotions might be denied to them on the basis of their gender. Following the gains made by women who earlier fought for women's rights like Harriet Tubman, Mary Ann Shadd, Nellie McClung and others, contemporary women accepted the challenge to improve women's situations. They began to determine ways to bring about changes in society that would improve their treatment, often starting with raising the awareness of women in respect to how they were being confined by expectations of society.

It was a time when Blacks dared to dream the impossible.

When the leader of the federal NDP, David Lewis, announced that he was retiring as leader in 1974, Rosemary was approached by supporters to run for the leadership of the national party. Rosemary declared that she would run for the leadership on a platform which included socialism, feminism, protection of the environment and the rights of workers and people to live in a fair and safe society.

Rosemary came to her feminism through her socialism. Her political activity is based on a commitment to feminism. And her commitment to feminism helped her to get women's support for her leadership campaign. Rosemary still views the leadership race as a milestone in her political life. It happened at a time when , as she says, "Blacks dared to dream the impossible: the possibility of a Black Canadian being a national political leader".

FEMINISM

A feminist believes that most societies treat men preferably to women, make it easier for men to succeed than women, that the whole social system established by men helps to keep most of the advantages for men. A feminist tries to challenge this advantage by not succumbing to the roles created for women by men but by creating her own role and by helping to change the stereotyped roles of a person's gender. This makes it acceptable for a woman to be an engineer and for a man to be a nurse, if this is what they want to be.

Because of her loyalty to the provincial NDP, Rosemary declined an offer to run as a candidate in the federal election that followed. Through re-organization of the electoral boundaries, her riding ceased to exist and she had to run in Burnaby-Edmonds, a suburb of Vancouver, to maintain a seat in the provincial government. This caused a great deal of stress for the family and was only relieved by Rosemary and Bill, without the children, moving to Burnaby when she was pressured to live in the area she hoped to represent.

The new riding of Burnaby-Edmonds had voted NDP consistently over the years and Rosemary found the staff in the riding office to be dedicated and hard working, enabling her to take on other responsibilities. She began to devote more of her time to international peace and development and represented Canada at the "Women for a Meaningful Summit Organization" and at a dinner to honour Bishop Tutu in Toronto. In 1987, Rosemary met her "special" role model, Angela Davis, at an international women's conference on peace. After ten years in provincial politics it was time for her to retire from politics and not run in the next election.

Shortly after this, she was notified that she had been appointed to the Ruth Wyn Woodward endowed Chair in Women's Studies at Simon Fraser University, Harambee, a national Black organization, established a fund for gifted Black children in honour of Rosemary, and she has received honorary degrees. She also accepted an appointment as Executive Director of MATCH International, a development agency that matches the expertise of Western women with the needs of Third World women.

In the summer of 1993, Rosemary was appointed the Chief Commissioner of the Ontario Human Rights Commission for a three-year term. At the same time, she was appointed by Parliament to be a member of the Security Intelligence Review Commission for a five-year term. In this way, her interests in fighting racism and sexism could be combined with her commitment to peace with a global perspective.

Rosemary has made a difference through her commitment to feminist ideals in a political environment. Her initiative in running for the leadership of the national New Democratic Party provided an example of courage to others who followed. She has contributed to the debate and policy making that have changed people's lives.

SYLVIA SWEENEY

Film Producer, TV Journalist, Musician, Composer,
Former,. Olympic Athlete for Canada,
President of her own Company (Elitha Peterson Productions)

BIRTH: OCTOBER 3, 1956 Montreal, Quebec

AS THE DAUGHTER OF ONE OF THE BEST MUSIC TEACHERS IN MONTREAL, and the niece of the world-renowned musician, Oscar Peterson, Sylvia might have been expected to do well at piano playing. She is an accomplished pianist but the fact that she has excelled in other areas as well is an indication of her dedication and hard work. Her achievements have ranged from being nominated the Most Valuable Player in the world for basketball, playing for Canada in the Olympics, as host and anchor of a television program and producer and director of films, including the acclaimed "In The Key Of Oscar". Sylvia likes to feel constantly challenged and takes educated risks to satisfy her curiosity and her craving to explore and learn new areas.

THE EARLY YEARS

Sylvia's father, James Sweeney, had immigrated to Montreal from Montserrat in the West Indies and her mother, Daisy Elitha Peterson Sweeney, was born in Montreal the daughter of parents who originally had come from St. Kitt's and the Virgin Islands. From the earliest years, music had been a part of the family's life. Because her mother taught piano from the Sweeney home, there were always people coming in and out of the house and there was always music being played on each of their four pianos. Sylvia's father was a cook on the railway and, therefore, he was away from home a great deal, leaving most of the discipline of Sylvia , her 3 sisters and 3 brothers to their mother.

Each week from Monday to Friday, when her father was away at work on the railway, the family home was a music studio and Sylvia was required to practice every morning, and often after school. Sylvia began to play the piano at the age of three and entered her first music competition when she was only five years old. From that age until she was eighteen, Sylvia's life was spent preparing for annual music events, including the McGill music exams and the Kiwanis Festival. In the summer, the Sweeney family would usually travel to Toronto to visit with Daisy's brother, Oscar Peterson , and his family to hear about Oscar's experiences on his concert tours around the world playing with notable jazz musicians.

Sylvia Sweeney

In addition to music, Sylvia's mother instilled in all her children a sense of responsibility for their actions. They could not use their

Uncle Oscar Peterson with Sylvia in his arms

"colour" as an excuse because prejudice, discrimination and racism would only handicap anyone who exhibited them. Her mother strongly felt that there was no reason for her children not to be the best that they could be. She knew that others, in their primarily White neighbourhood, had difficulty with the colour of her children and their height. She expected it so she armed her children with the will to exceed their personal standards despite the expectations from the community that they would not succeed. There was no excuse for not achieving. Daisy was also concerned about other people and instilled a sense of caring for other people in her children.

As the second youngest child in a large family, Sylvia could not go anywhere without a reason, so she often used her brothers and sisters as reasons. On one occasion, 12-year old Sylvia was with an older sister who was trying out for a local basketball team. The coach saw Sylvia, who was then 170 cm and asked her to join the team. For the next number of years, basketball became Sylvia's athletic and social life.

Sylvia had excelled in school and she was "fast tracked" into a special music program in piano performance at McGill University. She entered university at 17 and would later complete her Bachelor of Arts degree, at Laurentian University, study communications at Concordia University, Italian at Universita del Staniere (Perugia, Italy), Journalism at Holmesglen College (Melbourne, Australia) and cello at Conservatoire de musique de Quebec. Among her accomplishments is the fact that she is now fluent in three languages - English, French and Italian.

In basketball, her coach, Jack Donahue, gave her some good advice when he told her she was "different" and that she ought to use the opportunities that sports could provide after she had proven herself on the basketball court. To this day, she feels that sports is "an excellent environment for a child if it is a blending of fellowship with guidance" and that coaches need to be able to deal with the fun and the issues of growing up, just as a parent might. Also, there is the need to understand the goals that have been established. She feels that one should "use sport as a vehicle, not a destination". The fame, travel and contacts that are made through sports are invaluable but it is important to be well-rounded and develop your own broader interests. She recalls being criticized by some people for not being focused, as she continued to find time to play the piano instead of perhaps going out with the friends on the team. But her interests could include many different areas. She had been warned to use the opportunities and she was determined not to let sports use her.

MOST VALUABLE PLAYER

When the Quebec Provincial Basketball Team was touring high schools looking for young women to join the team, Sweeney's coach at school suggested that she try out. She made the team and two years later, in 1974, Sylvia had joined the National basketball team, and she stayed with the team for ten years. In 1976, she was selected to play for the Canadian Olympic team at the Montreal Olympics. Unfortunately, Canada boycotted the Olympics in 1980 but in 1984 she again played for Canada at the Olympics in Los Angeles. In 1979, at Korea, Sylvia was voted the Most Valuable Player in the World while playing for Canada's National Team. This was a highlight of her career in basketball and she is justly proud of her achievements. Increasingly, basketball provided her with physical challenges and gave her a chance to meet people, while playing the piano provided her with relaxation and another avenue in which to excel.

When Sylvia was named the Most Valuable Player in basketball, offers flowed in from around the world for her to play and coach. At the same time, she was accepted into Law School at McGill University. Sylvia decided to accept an offer to play professional basketball at Clermont Ferrand, France, the first Canadian to do so. The playing schedule was light and she was able to convince the President of the Association Sportif Montferrandaise to arrange for a piano for her and a job with her sponsor Michelin. After two years in France, the problems of the league forced all those who were foreigners to be sent home.

After travelling briefly with a regrouped Olympic team in 1982 for an exhibition tour, Sylvia accepted a contract with the best women's league in the world in Italy. Soon the political situation in

McGill University Basketball Team

Italy, and the risk to her safety made Sylvia relieved to leave Italy in 1983. Already on the Olympic team, she returned to Canada and continued as captain with coach Doug McRae in 1984. McRae had been the coach at the University of Waterloo and had gained international experience. Sylvia enjoyed working with the team and particularly with McRae and when he was abruptly fired by Basketball Canada without explanation Sylvia and some others demanded to be given the reason for his dismissal. The team decided that they would not play until they were told why McRae had been dismissed and as a result eight players walked off the team in protest.

Sports gives a false perception of what the world is about — Work does not.

Still not satisfied with this action, Sylvia investigated the financial statements of Basketball Canada and was surprised to learn that $2 million was supposed to have been spent on the team since McRae had been with them. She went to the media, and, in particular, the Canadian Broadcasting Corporation (CBC), to try to get them to ask about this as she questioned that such a large amount had been spent; and she and her teammates were successful in opening up an investigation into the whole matter. The Minister of Sport became involved, and an arbitration board was set up, which finally concluded that the coach, in fact, had grounds to sue for wrongful dismissal, and McRae was reinstated as coach. They succeeded in getting McRae back, but by the time the affair was over "everyone had changed", as Sylvia says, and team morale and momentum had been affected negatively. However, her leadership was recognized and she was offered a research position at CBC. She stayed in that position only for a couple of months before leaving to take advantage of an opportunity to play basketball in Australia.

Pan Am Games, 1983
Canada vs. Venezuela

Once securely a part of the Australian team, Sylvia again sought a job to satisfy her interests. Because of her experience, she became the Administrator of the Cobourg Basketball Stadium, in Melbourne. Basketball was just beginning to become popular of the Australia in 1984 and Sylvia wanted to sponsor a major event that would bring attention to the game and broaden its appeal in the country. In thinking about how to do this, she recalled an experience that she had while in Triesta, Italy, where the 12 best players in the world formed a team. For Sylvia, it was the most fantastic moment in sports as she finally had the chance to play with an entire team of people who were at the same level as she was. She decided to do the same in Australia and proceeded to raise the necessary money, find a suitable facility and contact the

In China, on tour, visiting the Great Wall

best players in the country to join and all-star team. It was a highly successful event and the event even made money. Because of her efforts, basketball is now a major spectator sport in Australia.

BRANCHING OUT

Finally, Sylvia felt it was time to retire from sports and she returned home to Montreal, where she was promised a permanent, not contract, full-time position as a sportscaster on television. However, because of budget cuts, it was not possible for her to be given a permanent position with the CBC , but as an alternative she was offered a contract position and she was able to fill in as a sports anchor on a regular basis. As a reporter on sports, her interest was more on the background of the people in sports, involving human interest aspects, rather than simply reporting on a sporting event. This interest came to the attention of Karl Nerenberg, the senior producer for current affairs at the CBC, and he was instrumental in giving Sylvia some journalistic, investigative reporting assignments. Sylvia credits him with being her best teacher at CBC because of his honesty in reporting.

She noticed that Societe Radio Canada, the French-language radio station of the CBC, had no "diverse groups" represented among its staff and coincidentally she was invited to be a member of a panel to discuss the issue of new immigrants to Canada. During the media conference "Eux et Nous", Sylvia challenged a number of stated stereotypes of new immigrants and she even offered to give her job to another panelist who expressed negative views of ethnic groups, "if he could show that his family had done more to contribute to the fabric of this country" than her family had done. With the accomplishments of her family, the opposition panelist had to concede. Shortly after this, Sylvia was appointed the Vice President of the Federation of Professional Journalists and with that position she lobbied to make hiring changes at the radio station so that there would be equal opportunity of employment for all minority groups.

Whenever anything gets to be 'old hat' I have to go on to something new.

Sylvia continued her interest in sports by coaching an amateur basketball team and serving as Assistant Athletic Director of Concordia University for a fund-raising project. Bob McDevitt, a colleague at the CBC in Montreal understood her feeling about wanting new challenges and advised her that she should consider becoming a producer. This recognition of Sylvia's potential and capabilities was meaningful to her and would give her an opportunity to expand in a direction that would suit her perfectly. She was not able to take up the profession of a producer immediately, but she did store the suggestion for a later time while she began to make it known that she would be interested in becoming a producer. The program, "CBC Newswatch", needed a musical theme and she composed and performed all the instruments for the theme of the program. With her high energy and enthusiasm, she put everything into her work. She began to work as a freelance producer with Radio Canada, anchored the weekend news on CBC, taught a course in journalism on the Kanehsatake Mohawk Territory near the town of Oka, Quebec, and taught a course in media at Dawson College. She established her own production company, Elitha Peterson Productions and she managed a band, Tchukon, that went on to win the "Star Search" TV program on NBC in the United States in 1986. Sylvia successfully managed all these activities at the same time: a work load that speaks to her discipline, creativity and initiative.

Following one of her classes in journalism, a band council member approached her and enquired about how to get the media to pay attention to the tensions that existed in 1989 between the Native Peoples and the town of Oka. The Mohawk peoples of Kanehsatake had resisted the intrusion into their tribal lands by a group who wanted to put in a golf course on their hallowed land. The stand-off lasted through the summer of 1990 and the cause of the Native People of Oka won support throughout the world. Sylvia, who feels that "if something isn't in the mainstream, it tends to be ignored", discussed with a council member the need to do something similar to what Martin Luther King, Ghandi or Socrates had done, a non-violent demonstration. They needed to answer the question: "Why should people care?" The stand off at Oka made people care. Sylvia also brought the story to "W5" who told her that "nobody cares about stories about Native Peoples", and she was not able to interest the media in the Oka demonstration at an early stage. When the Oka tensions finally erupted in 1990, Sylvia was on assignment in Vancouver for CTV's television program "W5", while some of her former students in the journalism course were behind the barricades at Oka. On her return from Vancouver, she tried to get behind the lines and report the situation, but she was not allowed to do so. Later, she was in a similar position of anticipating the political unrest and fall of the government in Romania, but the team was not allowed to report from that country, instead they had to cover events in Czechoslovakia. As well, a research document she prepared on the Ethiopian famine and Canada's involvement with it was "lost" and she was told that she did not understand the show and she was told only to suggest sports and music spots. Eventually, she left the program as it was time to look for new challenges.

BACK TO HER FAMILY ROOTS

Realizing that the story of her uncle, Oscar Peterson, had never been told on film, she conceived the idea of producing the film through her own production company, Elitha Peterson Productions, which had been named after her mother. It would be the story of his life entitled "In the Key of Oscar". She embarked on the planning of the film, but it would cost a lot of money and so she proceeded to try to raise the required $1 million to complete the project. At first she could not find any source of funding for that large amount of money and it looked as though the project would not be completed. She had thought of a number of avenues for the financing, but it wasn't until she approached George Cohon, chairman of McDonalds Restaurants of Canada, that she was able to get an important beginning in her quest for financing for the film. He gave her $25,000 to cover the costs of the first "shoot", and because of that she was able to approach the National Film Board and the CBC to raise more money. Her business partner, Sara Levinson, had a good contact in Sam Hughes. Sam and his wife Martha Blackburn, owner of CFPL, the London *Free Press* and president of the Blackburn Group, invited Sylvia to a party and Sam announced to his guests that the production needed financial support. Sylvia was committed to the film about her uncle and persisted, raising additional financial backing. Sam, Martha and Sylvia became friends, but, sadly, Martha died suddenly and her efforts are remembered in the closing credits of the film.

OSCAR PETERSON

Peterson is a world-renowned jazz musician and composer. He was born in Montreal and his early piano lessons were given by his sister, Daisy, Sylvia's mother, and he later studied with the classical pianist, Paul de Marky. In the 1940s, he won the Ken Soble amateur show and appeared on national radio programs, as well as being signed by RCA Victor Records.

In 1949, Peterson first appeared with the all-star "Jazz at the Philharmonic" at Carnegie Hall in New York produced by Norman Granz. Since then, he has performed around the world and has played with countless famous jazz musicians, including the legendary trio with Ray Brown (bass),and Herb Ellis (guitar). Throughout his career, Peterson has won numerous awards, including Grammies, *Playboy* "Best Jazz Pianist" and *Downbeat* awards. He was made a Companion of the Order of Canada in 1984 and has received honorary degrees from over 10 universities in Canada and the United States. His compositions include the "Canadian Suite"and his "Hymn to Freedom", which became a crusade hymn of the civil rights movement in the United States.

Education is most important to Peterson. In 1991 he was appointed Chancellor of York University in Toronto where he has given classes in performance and composition. He has founded the Advanced School of Contemporary Music in Toronto and the Oscar Peterson Opportunity Awards to provide financial assistance to high school students who have potential for university studies. The Oscar Peterson Scholarship has been established in his name by the famous Berklee School of Music, in Boston. He continues his commitment to education as well as developing his music through performances, composition and recording.

In the process of planning, researching, filming, editing and producing "In the Key of Oscar", Sylvia learned even more about how to handle responsibility since she often had to do unfamiliar tasks. She had to make arrangements herself, such as the time she had to arrange for a train to take the entire Peterson family to Montreal for the reunion scene of the film, or the time she had to find old film footage of her internationally respected uncle. During the course of the filming, she was able to reunite a previously unknown relative with Oscar, his half-brother whom she had met

Sylvia and her Uncle during the television production of "In the Key of Oscar".

earlier while in Vancouver on assignment. Throughout his career, Oscar Peterson had to travel extensively around the world and this had cost him a lot in terms of his family life and, through the filming, Sylvia was able to bring the family together. Sylvia, armed with this knowledge, and affected by the untimely death of her friend Martha, has acknowledged the need to excel but above all to have perspective about a balanced, well-rounded life.

At times, particularly in the early days, the fast-growing Elitha Peterson Production company needed money that they didn't have to complete other productions. To help raise the money, Sylvia would accept work outside her company. In one of these, she was invited to head the Women's section of the Ontario Ministry of Tourism and Recreation. Her responsibilities were to decide which groups should receive funding for their programs and she developed a new decision-making model to determine the criteria for judging proposals. Her model, based on how organizations tend to operate, tied funding to programs that would involve everyone was well received.

If I ever failed, I knew I had a family behind me. If you have a cushion, you can jump higher.

With the acceptance of the Bitove group to bring an NBA Basketball team to Toronto, Sylvia was asked to become a member of the Board of Directors of that organization as she could bring to this new organization her experience as an international basketball player, her knowledge of relations with the media and her creativity.

Sylvia has been motivated to work hard because of the strong support of her family. She has always been able to reach for high goals because of this. She continues to work on a number of film projects based on her interests and some cooperative ventures with other film makers. After completion of "In the Key of Oscar", she has worked on a number of projects, including a 4-part mini-series, "Hymn to Freedom", on the contributions of Blacks to Canadian society, and "The Finish Line," the story of Ben Johnson. Sylvia is absorbed in her work and if she has any regret, it is that she does not take enough time for herself.

Sylvia has made a difference because she has promoted fairness, equality and intelligence. She has been a leader and will continue to make a difference because of her commitment to excellence and her dedication to achieving.

OTHER BIOGRAPHIES

ZANANA AKANDE: Teacher, Consultant, Interviewer, Politician - Member of Provincial Parliament. Born in 1937 in Toronto, Ontario.

During the early years of her marriage to her husband, Isaac, an optometry student, and the arrival of her 3 children, Zanana's commitment to hard work and family values as well as her interest in the Black community was paramount. By the time that Isaac had become Dr. Akande, Zanana was well established in her teaching career and soon became an educational consultant. Zanana was interested in helping new Canadian children of primarily Black Caribbean families cope with the school system in the City of York and was instrumental in adapting testing procedures to be more reflective of their non-Canadian origins so that they were being assessed on their knowledge level rather than their understanding of their newly adopted culture. Zanana designed, developed and administered programs for other students needing special services, including the gifted and slow learners. Returning to the classroom, she went on to become a principal and later taught at University of Toronto and York University in the area of teacher-education.

She has been honoured for her involvement with the Federation of Women Teachers Association of Ontario by being presented the FWTAO Award in recognition of dedicated service to education in Ontario. Zanana is the co-founder of a magazine for visible minority women called "Tiger Lily" , the co-host of the Toronto Arts Against Apartheid Festival, and, was an interviewer for Multicultural Television (MTV). Zanana has served on the boards of several social services, including the United Way of Greater Toronto.

When the New Democratic Party formed its first government in Ontario, Zanana was elected in the riding of St. Andrew-St. Patrick in Toronto. She was appointed the first Black woman member of provincial parliament and the first Black woman cabinet minister. Appointed Minister of Community and Social Services, she was now responsible for provincial policies that affected the disadvantaged or people who needed assistance with financial, family or other situations. Sadly, Zanana's own family situation changed with the news that her husband was seriously ill. She resigned from politics to be with him, and after his death, helped to establish the Dr. Isaac Akande Educational Fund through the Black Business and Professional Association.

Upon her return to active politics, Zanana served as the parliamentary assistant to Premier Bob Rae and was responsible for the Jobs Ontario Youth program, which created some 10,000 summer jobs. In addition to her Committee work with Justice and the Ombudsman, her involvement with the Cabinet Roundtable on Anti-Racism led to the adoption of anti-racism programming in educational curriculum. Zanana is actively involved in helping to bring about changes to improve our society.

JEAN AUGUSTINE: Educator, Administrator, Politican. Born on September 9, 1936 in St. George's, Grenada.

Through the example of Jean's family and sharing and interacting with the community, Jean learned the value of giving of one's time and she developed a sense of social responsiblity. As her grandmother would often say, "To whom much is given, much is expected". Jean decided to become a teacher and she was put into the classroom with minimal training. When Jean later was hired as a teacher in Grenada, salaries were low. In exploring possibilities for university education abroad, Jean realized that it would take her a long time to save enough money for the costs of moving and paying tuition. Canada had a domestic-service program directed at Caribbean and other women who could be hired as nannies and housekeepers. Jean arrived in Canada in 1961 and was encourgaged by her employers to continue her education and she went on to earn her Masters in Education. Jean excelled in teaching and continued her studies, becoming a principal.

Her work with the community as a Board member with organizations addressing the needs of chidlren, justice and women, including her position as the national president of the Congress of Black Women of Canada, brought her to the attention of David Peterson, leader of the provincial Liberal party, and he asked her to join the party as a member of his transition team when the Liberals took power. In 1988, Jean was appointed to chair the Metro Toronto Housing Authority with a budget of $200 million. She advocated the improvement of the 154 housing projects for tenants by various means, including the development of an anti-drug campaign. She was later appointed to the Board of Governors of York University . In 1993, Jean was elected to the House of Commons as a Liberal member.

SALOME BEY: Singer, Actor, Composer, Recording Artist. Born in Newark, New Jersey.

One of nine children of a very musical family, Salome won her first award for singing by the age of 14 at the legendary Apollo Theater in New York City. The Apollo Theater was in Harlem and had a reputation for Black music excellence, and, many internationally famous Black performers had their first major talent competitions at the Apollo. Winning the Apollo's talent contest meant that you could perform there for a week, but Salome was not allowed to because her parents thought she was too young. Time passed, and Salome entered Law School at Rutger's, but she was still drawn to singing. She left her second year to become a full time entertainer, forming a vocal group with her brother , Andy, and sister, Geraldine, "Andy and the Bey Sisters". They sang in local clubs and soon started touring North America and Europe. Salome came to Toronto in 1964 and met her future husband, Howard Matthews.

Salome launched a solo career in the jazz clubs around Toronto, and made her theatre debut in 1969 at the Global Village in "Blue S.A." and "Justine". The latter piece was retitled, "Love Me, Love My Children" and went to New York during the 1971-1972 season where Salome won the prestigious OBIE Award as Best Actress for her Earth Mother role. She then spent two years on the road with the musical production "Don't Bother Me, I Can't Cope" and a year on Broadway with "Your Arms too Short to Box With God", winning a Grammy nomination for her work. Despite her success, she longed to have a role that was less emotionally draining and that would allow her to remain in Toronto with her husband and children.

By 1979, "Indigo", a jazz and blues cabaret show, played extended runs to sold-out audiences. Salome had put the show together to tell the story of the history of Black music. For her outstanding performance, Salome was awarded the Dora Mavor Moore Award, as was the show itself. "Indigo" was later taped and sold to the Arts and Entertainment Network in the United States for viewing worldwide. Salome went on to create and perform in two more shows based on the lives of Ethel Waters and Ma Rainey. Another dramatic musical is based on questions that her daughters asked her about drugs, love and other issues of concern to young people, "There ought to be a law replacing drugs with hugs" is one of the lines from that production, "Songs From A Rainbow World".

Salome has used her contralto range to good effect on many radio and television specials, she has appeared with other world class entertainers, including Dan HIll, Bill Cosby, the Donald Byrd Quintet, Anne Murray. She has been awarded three Cheer Black Music Awards and was one of Canada's musical ambassadors to Expo '92 in Seville, Spain. A recipient of the Toronto Arts Award for "her contribution to performing arts", she has made a difference as a powerful international performer with a universal musical message of love.

MARION ARETHA BORDEN: Religious Leader, Youth Pastor, Counsellor and Educator. Born on June 27, 1968 in Halifax , Nova Scotia.

For some people to excel, they only have to focus on one skill, or interest, but Marion has found that focussing on her calling to religion and on her community interest allows her to do the positive and productive activities that she enjoys. In 1992, Marion completed a Master of Divinity, directly following her completion of her B.A. , at Acadia University. To honour her for her dedication and academic success, Marion was awarded with 16 scholarships and bursaries for her academic excellence.

Because of her energy and commitment, Marion continued to work , during her studies, as a Student Pastor at Windsor Plains, St. Thomas United Baptist Church (North Preston) and Tracadie United Baptist Church. Marion also managed to find time to volunteer her time with a number of organizations. She was a founding member and publicity chairperson of the International Student's Gospel Choir at Acadia University, past president and executive member of the African United Baptist Youth Fellowship of

Nova Scotia, president of the Acadia Caricom Society (Caribbean and Commonwealth), researcher for the Black Cultural Centre and Marion has been a guest speaker or delegate at many church functions and provincial social or educational conferences.

Since her graduation, Marion has volunteered as a counsellor with battered women, tutored in a reading support program and volunteers office skills to a community health clinic while on the board of Voices Black Theatre Ensemble. Marion has been employed as a Program Officer with the Public Service Commission and a Project Historian with the B.C.C. and as a Youth Support Worker in Dartmouth.

DR. RUTH EVELYN BROWN - JOHNSON: Archivist and Historian of Africville. Born in 1919 in Africville (Halifax), Nova Scotia.

Born a descendant of one of the founding families of Africville, Ruth helped to organize and promote the Mount St. Vincent University exhibition entitled, "Africville: A Spirit that Lives On" in order to correct any misconceptions about the destroyed Halifax settlement. As she has said, "People who hold land for 140-something years deserve some respect."

Ruth has further dedicated herself to her church and her community through her primarily voluntary efforts. She was the first woman district Chair of the African United Baptist Association and the Provincial Supervisor of the Youth Fellowship for eight years. She has been the church organist for almost 50 years and showed equal interest in directing the choir. Ruth was President of the Society for the Preservation and Protection of Black Culture in Nova Scotia, a Councillor with the Black United Front and Program Chairman for the Black Cultural Society - she even wrote the lyrics and the theme chorus for the B.C.S.

Ruth received an honorary degree from Mount St. Vincent University in 1991 and currently hosts a monthly television show for seniors entitled "Seniors in Action".

JOAN BUTTERFIELD: Artist. Born in Bermuda.

After immigrating to Canada, and viewing some examples of the 17th Century furniture decorating technique of decoupage, Joan felt that she could use the same effect in an application of fine art. To express her creativity, four or more copies of the same print are cut, shaped, layered and sculptured to produce the effect of depth and dimension from a flat surface.

With her themes specializing in African-American, Caribbean, and African scenes, Joan's work is of particular interest to "Blacks (who) need accessible icons of pride within their homes and their communities.". In Canada, Joan is often commissioned to produce works for prominent guest speakers and she has permanent displays in several Toronto area galleries. Since 1988 Joan has been signed to an exclusive agreement with a division of "Essence" magazine, an African-American magazine for women, after the president of "Essence Art" saw a piece of her work. Through "Essence Art", and a New York City "Art Expo" in 1989, Joan gained significant international recognition and assignments. Her work is now found in over 20 galleries in the United States and in a number of galleries in the Caribbean. She has used her creativity and her interest in her African ancestry to produce unique pieces of art reflecting subjects and scenes not readily found in the mainstream art world.

GERVAIS COLLINS: Educator and Founder of Black Heritage School. Born in Jamaica, West Indies.

When Gervais arrived in Calgary in 1968, she "froze her fingers, but not her heart" which has allowed her to go on to become a concerned educator in the Calgary community. A full-time resource teacher at Thorncliffe and Catherine Nichols Gunn Elementary School, she contributes her time during the evening and on weekends as the co-ordinator of the Black Heritage School, which she helped to found. Gervais is committed to helping her students to feel that they are a part of Canada, since many of her Black students have roots outside of the country. She does this through discussing role models of African descent, teaching skills in coping with name calling and making her students feel good about themselves. Because of her warm and friendly nature, Gervais is the kind of person who young people turn to for advice.

Gervais also helped to create the Caribbean Dance Group which later became the Caribbees Dancing and Singing Group. She used the music and lyrics to discuss West Indian culture with the young people in the group. The Caribbees now are popular performers around Calgary, having receptive audiences with senior citizen homes and on special celebrations such as Canada Day, Heritage Day and Carifest.

Gervais is the Vice-President of the Calgary Branch of the Congress of Black Women, was the Secretary of the Jamaican Canadian Association and she has helped to establish a women's netball club for Caribbean women. She has been awarded the YWCA of Calgary Women of Distinction Community Service Award for her efforts to meet a need for cultural enrichment in the Calgary area.

RITA COX: Librarian, Storyteller, Community Worker. Born in Trinidad, West Indies.

As a young library worker in Trinidad, Rita was "discovered" telling stories by internationally-known storyteller, Augusta Baker. Baker arranged for Rita to study children's librarianship under her guidance at Columbia University in New York. Returning to Trinidad with her degree, Rita decided to apply for a position in Toronto after she learned of the excellent reputation of the library system there. In Toronto, she moved from library to library, honing her professional skills and gaining a reputation as a storyteller.

In 1973, she became a children's librarian at Parkdale Library in a downtown, working class neighbourhood in Toronto. Within months, she was promoted to head librarian and she launched a local ethnic festival which packed the library's auditorium. Noting the needs of the community and wanting to make the library responsive, she established a community-information centre. In 1976, she initiated "Festival International", which placed the focus of each school month on a different racial or cultural group with activities including lectures, films, art exhibits, storytelling, puppet shows, music and food. This led to the formation of the Parkdale Intercultural Centre to help promote a sense of community and is supported by grants from government.

Parkdale Library now has books available in 23 languages and Rita is the founder, selector and administrator of the largest collection of Black and West-Indian materials of any public library in the system. She is credited with being a visionary within the library system because many of her early initiatives have now become standard library programs across Canada, such as the preschool hour, community parents groups, "Parkdale Project Read" - adult literacy, "Read Together" - children's literacy, and a computer-equipped literacy centre.

Rita is on the Board and is the past-chair of the Storytellers School of Toronto, a founder of Kumbayah - a festival of Black heritage and storytelling , and the National Association of Black Storytellers, U.S.A. She is a member of the Toronto Arts Council Literary Committee, City of Toronto Awards Committee, Advisory Committee of the Ontario Arts Council. She has written widely and performed internationally. Among her many honors, she has received the Canada Birthday Award, the Ontario Bicentennial Award, the City of Toronto Award of Merit, the Ontario Folk Arts Foundation Fellowship for Storytelling, the Kay Livingstone Award of the Congress of Black Women, the Ontario Library Association Children's Services Guild Award and she has been appointed to be the consultant for a Toronto/Sao Paulo, Brazil library project. She has received an Honorary Doctor of Letters from York University as recognition her work. Her activities have inspired many and her work has become the model for other libraries to follow.

CHARMAINE CROOKS: Athlete : World Class Sprinter - 200M, 400M, 800M. Born on August 8, 1962, in Mandeville, Jamaica.

As a newly wed resident of North Vancouver, Charmaine works as a marketing representative and motivational speaker. She loves working with children and is involved with a "stay-in school program" and speaks on nutrition, fitness and health issues. Charmaine's interest in fitness started almost as she arrived in Canada with her family at age 6. She started competing by age 10 and joined the Canadian National Team and the Canadian Olympic Team by the time she was 18. Her brother, Natty, is a former National Team high jumper.

During her first international competitions in 1980, she set a sprinting record in the 400 metre, establishing the Canadian Junior Record with a time of 52.33 seconds. She established six more Canadian Junior or Senior Records, including 3 in the 4-by-400 relay and 3 in the 800 metre. Charmaine consistently placed among the top at track meets. By 1983, Charmaine set a Pan-American Games record in the 400 metre with a time of 51.49 seconds. In 1990 when she first attempted to compete in the 800 metre, under the supervision of coach Doug Clement, she placed first. When Charmaine entered the 800-metre event at the Goodwill Games in 1990, she became the first Canadian woman to break the two-minute mark with a time of 1:58.72. She has been ranked 5th in the world in the 800 metre and 6th in the 400 metre by "Track and Field News".

Charmaine has been honoured with the Sport Excellence Award in 1982,1983, 1984 and 1987; the Olympic Champion Award in 1985; and she was named UTEP's Female Athlete of the Year in 1983 and 1985. In 1991, she received the Johnny F. Bassett Memorial Award for displaying a combination of sporting excellence and commitment to the community.

VIOLA DESMOND: Teacher, Hairdresser, Noted for her role in race relations. Born on July 6, 1914, in Halifax, Nova Scotia and died on February 7, 1965 in Halifax.

Viola was trained originally as a teacher, but when her husband Jack lost an eye in a construction accident, they both took training in hairdressing so that they could work together in a combined hairdresser/barbershop on Gottingen Street in Halifax. Viola wanted to be near Jack to support him if required. In 1945, Viola won the Orchid School of Beauty Trophy and the childless couple were managing very well.

In 1946 on a business trip, Viola's car developed trouble on her way through New Glasgow, so she decided to go to a movie while the car was being repaired. Buying her ticket, she proceeded into the Roseland Theatre and took a seat on the main floor. But to her amazement, she was soon arrested. What Viola did not know was that in New Glasgow, Blacks were required to sit in the balcony, because of the "socially accepted" practice of segregation, and pay a lower admission price, while Whites paid slightly more and could sit on the main floor. She did not know about this local requirement, but offered to pay the difference in the cost of the ticket so that she could sit on the ground floor. However, she was arrested and was kept in jail overnight, without being allowed to consult a lawyer, and fined $25 and court costs. Viola had been convicted of defrauding the government of Nova Scotia the tax difference between the cost of a main floor and a balcony seat, representing, a total of 19 cents.

Like Rosa Parks in the United States and her connection to the social change sparked by the Montgomery Bus Boycott and the subsequent march on Washington led by Dr. Martin Luther King, Viola Desmond made a difference because her situation similarly propelled people into action. Viola's dreadful experience in New Glasgow as an innocent single act occurred before the Rosa Parks incident. Because of Viola's treatment, Blacks who had not known of the seating practice at theatres in Nova Scotia, as well as those who were angrily searching for a way to end it joined forces. Many Black organizations developed in Nova Scotia and through their lobbying, petitions, questioning and other political activity, they were able to bring about an end to Nova Scotian segregation by 1954. Viola Desmond made a difference because of what she represented to a Black community that "wasn't going to take it anymore" and to others committed to equality for all.

DOLLY GLASGOW-WILLIAMS: Community Worker and Counsellor. Born in East Preston, Nova Scotia.

Active as one of the 16 children of Aubrey and Hilda (Taylor) Glasgow, Dolly learned the value of participating in her environment at an early age. Earning her high school diploma, she later began to attend St. Mary's University part-time, taking courses in law and business. She plans to work toward a degree in Business Administration. Married to Sinclair Williams, they have five children and three grandchildren.

First qualified as a seamstress, Dolly went into nursing, before leaving to study for her Certificate in Business. She has been employed with the province of Nova Scotia for over 18 years.

Dolly is very active in her community as a list of 50 of her positions and involvement's covers only some of her accomplishments. Dolly has been an executive member of a number of organizations; she was appointed by Cabinet to the Provincial Health Council of Nova Scotia. Dolly is a past-executive member of the National Congress of Black Women and president of a provincial chapter. Dolly was honoured by the YWCA in 1989 for her outstanding community work. As a board member of the Coalition Against Apartheid, Dolly joined a delegation meeting held by Nelson Mandela in Toronto in 1990.

In January 1993, Dolly was elected president of the Black United Front of Nova Scotia.

Dolly is a tireless, dedicated community worker who finds the time to encourage and support her peers while juggling a schedule of meetings and appointments that require precision planning. She is personable and committed to beneficial changes in society.

SYLVIA HAMILTON: Filmmaker, Writer, Journalist. Born in Nova Scotia.

With her primary interest in women of African descent in Nova Scotia, Sylvia has undertaken a number of creative and artistic projects to highlight her research and to share her discoveries. Sylvia has written poetry, essays, scripts and teacher guides. She has given numerous presentations about Black people, especially women and youth. She has worked for the National Film Board as a Program Consultant and filmmaker; as a reporter/broadcaster for several radio stations and as the acting regional director of the Department of the Secretary of State.

Despite these impressive accomplishments, it is Sylvia's filmmaking that has brought her international recognition. The film, "Black Mother, Black Daughter", focussing on the lives and experiences of several Black women in Nova Scotia, was researched, written, narrated and co-directed by Sylvia winning two awards after 40 festival screenings across Canada, the United States and Europe. These awards include the Margaret Mead Film Festival, New York, 1990, and the Museum of Modern Art, Documentary Film Program, New York, 1991. She has researched, written and directed an educational video about Black Loyalists, "The Bet: A Story of Black Loyalists in Nova Scotia", and a documentary film sharing the perspectives of Black youth entitled, "Speak it! From the Heart of Black Nova Scotia". Sylvia has also directed the Jones of Truro section of the 4-part "Hymn to Freedom" television series and is working on filmography projects dealing with racism and employment equity.

Sylvia has made a difference because she has been successful in helping others see with her eyes and feel with her heart about the issues that impact on Black people in Nova Scotia and therefore all people, especially those who are of African descent in Canada.

EDITH HENRY: Receptionist to Supervisor of Payroll. Born December 6, 1925, Springhill (now part of the City of Fredericton), New Brunswick.

Sometimes people make a difference and are inspiring examples to others, because of the personal obstacles that they have had to face on a daily basis. Edith is one of those people. Born the ninth of the ten children of Cecil Ernest and Charlotte Edna (Payne) Henry, her humble but happy childhood was invaded by a virus that left her physically challenged. Polio now made the two-mile walks to school impossible, and as a young woman she spent eight months in hospital receiving therapy that eventually allowed her to walk with braces. Determined to be independent, she moved to Boston to stay with her sister and received more treatment that improved her mobility. When she returned to Springhill in 1953, Edith attended Business College. She had to be assisted up the stairs everyday. She obtained a receptionist position with the Polio clinic in 1955, and ultimately became a Supervisor in the Payroll department of the hospital.

Edith's commitment to being a self-supporting, contributing person and her positive philosophy are evidence of the strength of the human spirit. That she was suggested as a woman who has made a difference shows that meeting personal obstacles is as admired as meeting social barriers - and Edith had both to confront as a Black, "disabled" woman.

NOLIE HERBERT: Community Work, Girl Guides, Women. Born in Bermuda.

Nolie came to Canada with her parents and brothers. She learned the importance of hard work, education and commitment to the community from them as her family grew and settled in Toronto and applied this to her own life. Married, later to be divorced, Nolie was responsible for raising her three children by herself: John, a musician, Carmen, a community worker and Ritchie, a professional hockey player.

By 1974, Nolie started to volunteer with the Girl Guides of Canada as a Lieutenant in Guiding, becoming a Guider-in-Charge by 1977. Nolie has held several division positions including Division and District Treasurer, Division Cookie Advisor, Department District Commissioner and Division Training Advisor. From 1990 to the present, Nolie has been a Pathfinder Guider in Charge and since

1992, the Division Camp Advisor which reflects the commitment of Nolie to spend most of her weekends and summers supervising campers at Girl Guides of Canada campsites. Nolie was awarded the long-term service award in 1989 for 15 years of service. On June 16, 1992, on a motion passed by Guide Council, Nolie became the youngest person ever to receive the Merit Award in Canada and one of the first Black women to be so honoured.

Nolie was introduced to the North York Chapter of the Congress of Black Women in 1986 and became a Vice President in 1987. Nolie manages to make everyone that she is working with feel that their contribution is important, and she is able to think of good ideas for activities or fundraising. At the regional level, Nolie is credited with constantly making suggestions to improve the status of women in all of the chapters. She is viewed as a person who will do more than she is expected to do, and who will manage to do it very well. Nolie became one of the first recipients of the Trilogy Award initiated by the North York Chapter for outstanding, dedicated volunteerism and was recommended by her Chapter to receive the Award of Merit of the Congress of Black Women of Canada. Nolie says of her volunteer work, "I consider my contribution a way of giving back to God. We should all help mankind anyway we can."

JENNIFER HODGE-DE SILVA: Film Producer. Born in Montreal, Quebec, and died on May, 1989,in Montreal, Quebec.

Jennifer, daughter by a former marriage of Mairuth Sarsfield, was educated in Switzerland. This multi-lingual woman, fluent in English, French and German, then sought her degree in Fine Arts from York University before obtaining her Television Arts Diploma from Ryerson Polytechnical Institute by 1979.

Jennifer began her film career in 1974 with items broadcast on CBC which were produced by Seawolf Films, a company of which she was a partner. She both edited and researched a documentary on the funeral of an Ashanti King in West Africa called "A Great Tree Has Fallen", edited two subject films on fishing villages in Ghana called "Jano, Elmina" and then directed "Seventy Cycles," about the World Bicycle Championship in Montreal. Her work on African themes helped her to express her interest in her own heritage as a person of African descent, but not as much as "Fields of Endless Day", the National Film Board film in 1978 in which she was the associate director. That film was nominated as "Best Documentary" by CFTA. This drama-documentary on the history of the Black community in Canada was one of the first films about Blacks in Canadian history made from the perspective of a Black Canadian. One of her last films, "Home Feeling : Struggle for a Community", 1983, came from her curiosity about why a woman was so afraid to let her daughter go out to play in the Jane-Finch area of Toronto, a multi-ethnic but largely Caribbean-Canadian community. The film is told from the perspective of West-Indian Canadians. Although it was never aired on television, the film was later used by police forces across the country to develop strategies for working with ethnic minorities. This theme had been previously touched upon in "Myself - Yourself", produced by Jennifer through her own production company, Jenfilms Inc. This film explored racial stereotyping in the educational system and won a Silver Medal at the New York International Film Festival and a Chris Plaque at the Mannheim Festival.

Jennifer directed or produced a number of other film projects, including "Dieppe 1942", which won the Prix Anik for Best Television Documentary at the Edinburgh Film Festival. She directed "In Support of the Human Spirit", a documentary on prison reform which won the Award for Creative Excellence at the 1987 United States Industrial Film and Video Festival. Married to filmaker Paul de Silva they had a daughter, they called Zinzi. Her continuing creative brilliance was lost to us when she died of cancer while in the process of developing a feature length screenplay, "No Crystal Stair", but the impact she had with her keen ability to use the camera to capture and convey feelings, not just ideas, will remain in her acclaimed works.

MARGUERITE JACKSON WILSON: Music Teacher, Secretary, Church worker. Born in July 1908, in Dresden, Ontario and died December 19, 1992, in Owen Sound, Ontario.

Perhaps the last of the traditional Black church women in Ontario, the British Methodist Episcopal Church was paramount in her life. Given the limited opportunities that society offered for Blacks at that time, a life spent in service to one's church was not uncommon and although not always profitable, it was prestigious to be a leader of the community. Born to The Right Reverend T. H. Jackson of the B.M.E. Church and his wife Laura, Marguerite survived a humble childhood to become an ardent church worker herself. Well known throughout Ontario because of the many times the family had to move to serve in different districts, Marguerite distinguished herself as a pianist and taught music to children.

As an adult, her family settled in Toronto and Marguerite became the Church Clerk, Sunday School Superintendent, President of the Missionary Society and she continued to teach piano. She would later become the founding President of the B.M.E. Senior Citizen Club, which extended to other churches. With the death of her father, Marguerite was left to care for her frail mother. At the time, there were no nursing homes for Blacks, and any other arrangements were not acceptable to Marguerite. She took a secretarial position with the Home Service Association, an organization serving the Black community with educational, day care and other services. She would have earned more working elsewhere, but her dedication to those sharing her heritage and her desire for a flexible job so she could care for her mother, prevented her from obtaining a more remunerative position. In 1975, Marguerite married Reverend Thomas Wilson. As a 67-year old newlywed, Marguerite moved to Owen Sound where her husband had been posted to the B.M.E. Church and the neighbouring church in Collingwood.

Marguerite made a difference because it is through the dedication, commitment, hard work and sacrifice of all of the people such as her that independent, Black churches and organizations are able to function. She made a difference because she volunteered her life's energy into supporting her family, her church family and her community.

MOLLY JOHNSON: Singer, Songwriter, Initiator of Kumbaya Festival. Born in Toronto, Ontario.

As a child of mixed heritage attending North Toronto's Brown Public School, Molly would defend her brown skin colouring by inventing incredible stories about her background in order to explain her presence as the only non-Caucasian child in the school. Her stories with the recurring theme, "I'm an Egyptian princess" would often prevent her classmates from leaving the schoolyard on time for their classes. Her early report cards branded her as "tenacious and incorrigible", qualities that still motivate her as an adult.

Her father was Black, university educated, and from the ghetto of Philadelpia, while her mother was White, on the social register and the daughter of a Supreme Court Judge from South Dakota. After their marriage, Molly's maternal grandparents acted as if their daughter, her mother, had died, and had no contact with the couple. Mrs. Johnson worked for CUSO (Canadian University Students Overseas), Voice of Women and has recently established Bruce House in Ottawa for AIDS victims. Mr. Johnson brought the family to Toronto to open YMCAs, was a player on the Philadelphia Eagles and later coached at Ryerson and Rochdale Colleges. Now divorced and remarried to other partners, her parents were instrumental in sparking Molly's social consciousness. Molly feels that everyone has a spark, the challenge is to ignite it in each individual.

Molly's brother, Clark, is an actor and he was born while their parents still lived in Philadelphia; her actor-singer-comedian sister, Taborah, was born while their parents lived in Switzerland and Molly was born in Canada. Her parents had a bohemian lifestyle and were, therefore, understanding of their children's wishes to follow careers in the arts. The children attended the National Ballet School. Situated in downtown Toronto, the school was near restuarants which attracted musicians and, as Molly saw her opportunities in ballet being limited because of her ethnic background, she again became involved in singing. Molly and her brother and sister had early theatrical and musical experience, appearing at the O'Keefe Centre and in CBC productions - Molly was 4-years old when she performed in "Porgy and Bess" and this contributed to her love of music by Gershwin, Cole Porter and Billie Holiday - whom her parents had known.

Ten years after her start in entertainment, she was voted "Most Promising Singer". She started out living above a coffee house, the Cameron, on Queen Street West , exchanging her services as the club's cleaning lady and resident singer with Blue Monday for free accommodation. One of her first performances as a singer was at the Imperial Room of the Royal York Hotel. In addition to the classic sounds of Gershwin, Ellington and Porter, Molly enjoys singing the music she has written with her music partner, Norman Orenstein. He has stayed with her while she performed with her group, Alta Moda, a high style, high art rock group and her current group, Infidels, a rock and roll band. "It's uniquely Canadian to mix cultures and mix sound in a musical group."

Using her musical ability, and contacts as well as her interest addressing the issue of AIDS, Molly worked hard at creating the "Kumbaya Festival" to raise money for the support of AIDS hospices across the country. Broadcast live in September 1993 from Ontario Place in Toronto by Much Music, the event was expected to raise $200,000 and still photographs from the concert were compiled into a calendar to raise additional funds. The concert featured, in addition to Molly, top Canadian performers, such as Murray McLaughlin, Tom Cochrane, Sandra Shamus, Randy Bachman, Crash Vegas, Rick Emmett and Rush, "because you can't get out there and play for those kids every night and not give them a message".

It is Molly's intention to ensure that this Festival becomes an annual event. She feels that talent and health are gifts. "It's a gift , and gifts are for sharing". The many benefits that Molly has done to help raise money for various causes show that she is willing to share, and lead the way to a new solution as much as she can. She hopes that her message to young people, the people who listen to her music, and the music of other contemporary performers, will be heard, because she is not sure that other messages encouraging safe sex are enough. It is her hope that young women especially will be motivated to "Stay straight and strong and true to yourself because you are responsible for your emotional and physical health. If we can't find a cure, then we can stop the spread of AIDS."

KAY LIVINGSTONE: Business woman, radio, television, and stage actor. Born in London, Ontario, and died in 1974 in Toronto, Ontario.

Kay's ancestors were from Cayuga and they moved into the London and Chatham area of Ontario. Her father, James Jenkins, was an Assistant Judge of the Juvenile Court in London and had founded, with her mother Christina, one of the earliest Black newspapers in Ontario, "The Dawn of Tomorrow". The contents of this paper, focussing on issues of the history and contributions of people of Blacks in North America, not only helped to make her father a community leader but it also had a deep impression on Kay which would forever make the positive activities of Black people important to her.

Kay's early education was in London, and she later excelled in Drama and Speech Arts at the Royal Conservatory of Music in Toronto, and the Ontario College of Music in Ottawa. Raised in a family that was dedicated to helping others, it was not surprising that she would work in service to her country. In Ottawa, as a civil servant, she married George Livingstone of Antigua, and, Kay hosted her own Ottawa radio program, "The Kathleen Livingstone Show", which featured music and poetry. They then moved to Toronto. While raising their family of five, Kay maintained her involvement with the performing arts and became one of Canada's leading Black actors of both the amateur and professional stage, television and film, and she had her own radio shows on CBC and CKEY in Toronto, and CFPL in London. With her "Kay Livingstone Show" on CBC, she focussed on the traditions and cultural activities of the African diaspora, or Black people of the world, since she was dedicated to promoting understanding of the contributions of Black people to Canadian society.

Kay's involvement in the community was impressive. She was the founding president of the Canadian Negro Women's Association, which lead the way for the formation of the National Congress of Black Women of Canada, Regional Chair of the National Black Coalition of Canada, Chair of the Canadian Council of Churches, president of the United Nations Association - Women's Section, on the Appeal Board of Legal Aid Society.

This well-known businesswoman, radio commentator and actor died suddenly in the process of working on a project to contact and join together all women of colour, to find strength and support in each other for their talents and contributions to society. Upon meeting community-activist, Dr. Carrie Best, the two became close friends. Carrie became the leader of the organization in Nova Scotia, and as a tribute to Kay, the organization became known as the "Kay Livingstone Visible Minority Women's Society". Kay's integrity and persevèrance ought to make everyone appreciate the efforts and energy of this woman for all Canadians.

REVEREND JEAN J. MARKHAM: Entrepreneur, Community Worker, Religious Leader Born in Barbados, West Indies.

Coming to Canada in 1957 to study Business Administration at Albert College in Belleville, Ontario, Jean completed her three-year course in just one year while fulfilling an appointment as counsellor in charge of her fellow students. Not wishing to return to Barbados earlier than expected, Jean applied to stay in Canada. Moving to Toronto, Jean attended St. Paul's Anglican Church until meeting a friend from Barbados who invited her to her church, the British Methodist Church of Canada, which had been established in 1856 and was owned and operated by Black Canadians. On her second visit, she noted that the organ was in need of repair; and so she asked the minister, Reverend Alexander S. Markham if it would be all right for her to raise the necessary funds. With his consent, she established a committee, and shortly thereafter, Jean not only had joined the church and repaired the organ, but she had met her future husband.

Jean was shocked to discover that she needed to have a man sign the contract for the organ repair, especially since she was the owner, manager and founder of her own businesses, Burke's Stenographic Services and Burke's Employment Agency. Jean was the first Black businesswoman since 1865 (Madame Augusta' dressmaking services) to provide professional services to the community. Jean went on to teach at Shaw's Business School, to be on the Teacher's Council of the Business Educator's Association of Canada and later to a career in real estate which gave Jean the flexibility she needed as the wife of the Presiding Bishop of the B.M.E. Churches. She served in several church offices and committees before her 1970 marriage to Reverend Markham, including trustee, secretary and treasurer, and she founded the Ladies League, edited both the "Rainbow" and the "Apostle" (the official voice of the church), chaired the committee which secured a historical designation for the Chatham birthplace of the B.M.E. and produced a record album of sacred music by the Toronto B.M.E. Church choir.

Jean decided to join her husband in the ministry, becoming only the second woman to be ordained in the B.M.E. church after Reverend Addie Aylestock. Jean suspended her studies for her Master of Divinity as she attended her husband in his declining health. Her husband died in 1988 and a year later, Reverend Jean Markham established a church in his name and she became it's pastor in 1990. Jean is also the founding National President of the Canadian Association of the Minister Wives and Ministers Widows organization, with it's headquarters in the United States and a membership of 33,000 women worldwide. Among her accomplishments in the community are the following, the first Regional Director of the (Ontario Division) Canadian Sickle Cell Society (honoured with a life membership), the founding Chairman of the Black Women's Support Group of the Canadian Mental Health Association (CMHA), and served on the Board of the CMHA.

BEVERLY MASCOLL: Entrepreneur, Co-Chair of the first Black Studies Chair (Dalhousie University). Born in Halifax, Nova Scotia.

Growing up as the only Black girl in the small town of Fall River, Nova Scotia, Beverly quickly had to learn how to defend herself against insensitive acts or racist comments. Learning how to cope was a difficult but valuable lesson for Beverly since it helped to prepare her to deal with all kinds of people and how to cope with rejection. And, people were not always courteous to the budding entrepreneur as she sold her hand-picked mayflowers and blueberries door-to-door to earn spending money. The wider world opened up to her as she travelled around the province to attend family or church function. She saw various Black communities and came to understand the need for taking action to create your own job opportunity.

Moving to Toronto in the 1950s, Bev accepted a job with Toronto Barber and Beauty Supply company becoming assistant to the president within six months. During her ten years at this office, she acquired a good basis in both the beauty and the business aspects of the company. Bev identified a gap in the beauty supply area, noting that there were no products available for the women of African descent. Bev decided to take a risk and meet this need on her own so she contacted the largest supplier of Black beauty products in the United States, then Johnson Products, and they allowed Bev to become their exclusive distributor in Canada. Bev recognized that stylists working with the new hair products would need special training so she provided product-based seminars. By now married to

Emerson, Bev began a new business, Mascoll Beauty Supply Limited, with a new baby and succeeded.

Because of her high profile in the business community, and her interest in raising self-esteem and Black History, Bev was asked to co-chair the fund-raising drive to support the first Chair in Black Studies from Dalhousie University. This travelling Chair, named after Nova Scotia's first Black lawyer – James Robinson Johnson, will have scholarships to benefit students in many communities across the country. Bev has served on many Boards including the Ontario Science Centre, Ryerson Polytechnical Institute and the Canadian Club. Among her honours are the Harry Jerome Award, the Canada 125th Medal and the Women of Distinction Award from the YWCA in 1993.

DR. PEARLEEN OLIVER: Community Worker, Religious Worker, Writer. Born on June 22,1917, in Halifax, Nova Scotia.

Had Pearleen continued to work hard by the side of her husband, who was a Minister, only the members of the Baptist Churches in Nova Scotia might know of her. But as Pearleen gained confidence serving on numerous Boards and Committees of her Church, and Pearleen and her husband, William, raised their 5 sons, she was moved to do what she could to make her church and her community more responsive to the needs of women. Within her church, Pearleen was responsible for initiating a Women's Institute which was launched in 1955 in the Cornwallis Street Baptist Church. It has grown in importance and is a provincial organization. Pearleen was later elected the first Woman Moderator of the African Baptist Association in 1976.

In the community, Pearleen became a founding member of the Nova Scotia Association for the Advancement of Coloured People, an organization which sought to improve the status of Blacks in Canada. During the 1940s, strong barriers existed which prevented Black women from being allowed entry into many training programs, including nursing. This became a crusade for Pearleen and she sought to change this situation by gathering information on the efforts of Black women to enter nursing and by a program of public speaking to share these difficulties with whomever would listen. Speaking as often as three times a week, she attracted such good publicity that within a year the Board of the Children's Hospital in Halifax asked Pearleen to send them two high school graduates, but the hospital would not guarantee their reception at other hospitals. Ruth Bailey of Toronto, who had previouly told Pearleen that she had attempted to get into nursing programs in every hospital in Canada but was refused because of her "colour", was accepted as was Gwen Barton of Halifax. Through their success at their studies and through Pearleen's efforts to have them enrolled, the discrimination against Black women in nursing ended in Canada.

Noting the success of her N.S.A.A.C.P. speaking campaign, Pearleen next attacked the racial slurs and demeaning references to Blacks in school books, such as Little Black Sambo, which stopped being used by 1950 because of her efforts. On her own, Pearleen collected hundreds of artifacts on the Black Baptist churches in Nova Scotia for over a two-hundred year period and donated the collection of documents and pictures to the Black Cultural Centre in Dartmouth. Pearleen also volunteered with the YWCA, the Maritime Home for Girls (Truro), the Board of the N.S. Cancer Society, the Black United Front and Canadian Girls in Training. She has written on the history of the Coloured Baptists and other articles for religious magazines. Pearleen continues to serve as the organist of her church and has done so for 34 years.

Among her many distinctions, Pearleen has received many plaques and certificates from youth, the community and church groups, including the Presidents Award of the Black Cultural Centre, an award by the Congress of Black Women, an honorary Doctor of Letters from St. Mary's University in 1990, where she had the privilege of being the first Black Nova Scotian woman to give the Convocation address, and her second honorary Doctorate from Mount St. Vincent in 1993. Pearleen's efforts have made profound changes in our country for everyone's benefit.

ANNE PACKWOOD: Teacher, Foster Parent, Community Worker, Actor. Born on April 7, 1898 in Bermuda.

George De Shield moved his family to Canada in 1908 when whaling was no longer able to support them. He immediately became a leader in Montreal's growing Black community, helping to found the Union Street United Church and the

Universal Negro Improvement Association (UNIA). His example inspired Anne and her sister Clara to do what they could to help. Anne taught kindergarten, was secretary for the UNIA Literary Club and the Debating Society, and organized and provided tutoring for Black children who had social problems to encourage them to remain in school and to help them develop a positive self image and pride in their race.

After her marriage and the births of her two daughters and adoption of one daughter, Anne was moved to provide foster care for children of mixed heritage who were rejected by other caregivers. Drawing from her knowlege and experience, Anne agreed to speak about the special needs of the multi-racial/multi-ethnic child in a radio series for CBC in the 1950s. In 1966, Anne had received an award form the City of Montreal to recognize her continuous care of children , beginning in 1926, which was the longest period of care provided by a foster parent of any racial background in Montreal.

During the 1940s and 1950s, Anne was drawn into acting by the Negro Theatre Guild, playing a leading role in their production of "Emperor Jones". She assisted her husband, Edward, to establish one of Montreal's first Black weekly newspapers, The Freelance. Among her many appointments, Anne was the longest-serving president of the Coloured Women's Club, which is the oldest Black organization in Montreal. For her outstanding work in the community, Anne was presented with a plaque and an award.

GRACE PRICE TROTMAN: Musician. Born on April 14, 1911, in Cape Palmas, Liberia. Died on March 8, 1982, in Toronto, Ontario.

Immigrating to Canada with her missionary parents in 1921, Grace was educated at the Royal Conservatory of Music, specializing in Negro Spirituals and Folk Songs receiving first class honors; she later graduated in Choir Directing. Grace was the organist and choir director of the B.M.E. Church for 40 years. She lead the choir to four successive first prizes in church music at the Kiwanis Festival. Her husband Colin was a renowned baritone, and one of her two children had a career in music.

She was a member of the Canadian Youth Congress, on the board of the Home Service Association, and she organized the Negro Youth Movement which presented the concerns of young people of African descent to City Hall. Grace also co-directed a camp for Black children which included a focus on Black History. Grace organized and directed the Negro Choral Group and its 70 members performed in the Toronto area to raise money for the War Victims Fund. Grace touched people in a more personal way as the music teacher of 30 pupils a year for over 40 years. Some of her students went on to become renowned in their own right, including Oscar Peterson the jazz pianist.

The only Black woman to be honoured with an "Outstanding Woman Award" as part of the International Woman's Year presentations by the province of Ontario in 1975, she also received other awards from her church, including the "Woman for a Better Canada Award". Her dedicated service to the church and the community indeed helped to make a better Canada.

JILLIAN RICHARDSON-BRISCOE: Athlete - World Class Sprinter (200M, 400M). Born on March 10, 1965, in Port of Prince, Trinidad, West Indies.

When Jillian was a four-year old girl in Trinidad, she had to try to keep pace with her mother as they made their way to school. Jillian recalls this as her first exposure to running, since her mother did not slow down to help Jillian stay in step. By 1977, Jillian and her family had moved to Calgary, Alberta, and Jillian's early "training" in running had prepared her for competitive running the following year. As a 13-year old her speed was remarkable and when she was 14 she placed first in the 200 metre at the 1980 Junior National Indoor Championships with a time of 25.55, later at the Junior National Outdoor Championships, she came first in the 400M with a time of 54.33 and was awarded the Canadian Track and Field Association's Myrtle Cook Trophy for Outstanding Junior Female Athlete of the Year.

Jillian continued to excel in her field placing first in the 200M in 24.78 seconds at the 1981 National Indoor Championships and first in the 400M in 54.45 seconds at the Canada Games. Joining the Canadian National Team in 1982, she continued to lead the way in sprinting, placing among the top at every international or Canadian meet in the 200M, 400M or 4 by 100 relay including the Harry Jerome Classic, Canada-China-Japan Junior Meet, Canada-U.S. Dual Meet, Pan

American Junior Meet and the 1983 West German International Meet where she set a Canadian Junior record for her 400M run in 51.91 seconds. She is a recipient of the Sport Excellence Award for 1983 and 1986, and the Olympic Champion Award, 1985, at the Tribute to Champions. Her personal best, under coach John Cannon's direction, for the 400M was set in 1988 at 49.91.

Now a wife and mother of a son, she is also a psychology student at the University of Calgary. Having recovered from severe injuries received in a traffic accident, in May, 1993, Jillian hopes her love of running and hard work will lead her to the first place podium at the 1996 Olympics in Atlanta. "I think it is important to know you did all you could do on a particular day. If I train hard, nobody is going to beat me."

SANDI ROSS: Actor, Founder of "Into the Mainstream". Born on January 23, 1949, at St. Paul, Minnesota, Minnesota.

Once, when Sandi was 4 years old and she found herself awakened by a thunderstorm, she commanded the heavens to "Stop that noise out there!". Sandi is the type of person who, when faced with incredible forces, challenges them. She says that she was lucky to have a mother who allowed her to take every kind of lesson possible. Sandi lived near the Tyrone Guthrie Theater in Minneapolis for several years, after having completed her Bachelor of Fine Arts degree, and was constantly made aware that there were good actors in Canada because they were frequently performing at this theatre. Sandi got a role with Theatre Calgary in the fall of 1976. By 1978 she had worked her way east to Toronto's St. Lawrence Centre. Although Sandi came to Canada for both love and work, as she puts it, "love left", but a new love, for Toronto and Canada developed, so Sandi stayed.

Sandi has been the principal actor in a number of film and television productions, including "Underground to Canada", "Tek War" and "Secret Service". She has performed in Shakespearean and contemporary theatrical roles such as "Twelfth Night" and "Streetcar Named Desire". Her list of acting roles takes several pages to document. Sandi has also directed and choreographed several productions, including "Closet Dancer" and "Bells are Ringing".

Sandi was elected to the Toronto branch of ACTRA, the national organization for all professional actors, in 1987 and she is now the Vice-President. As she became increasingly more involved with ACTRA and with other arts organizations and unions, she became interested in promoting visible minorities, audible minorities, (people with accents), and disabled performers because she felt there was a great deal of talent not being used. During a 1990 conference, "Into the Mainstream", a project of the same name was conceived to supply Canadian and international producers, directors and casting agents with a book designed to promote the diversity of talent within Canada.

With grant money, Sandi was able to found and edit Into the Mainstream, the only national book of it's kind to promote equity within the professional arts industry since "we - visible minorities, aboriginal people, European audible minorities and disabled- have all been marginalized by the mainstream, but working together, we can make changes" . Into the Mainstream is a pro-active talent directory, putting the faces of the underemployed into the hands of those who have the ability to employ them. This directory makes a difference because it promotes employment for certain groups and it is designed to bring in more international productions to Canada thereby benefitting everyone.

To honour Sandi for her work in creating and developing Into the Mainstream, she received the New Pioneers Award for the Arts. She dedicated the award to her late mother. Sandi's commitment to promoting professional actors most likely to be overlooked because they do not conform to a single image of beauty or ability has taken tremendous courage in an industry where physical characteristics are so closely connected with who gets the part. "If the so-called mainstream could work together as well as we do then there would be no need for Into the Mainstream", which is her personal goal.

BEV SALMON: Nurse, Arbitrator, Politician. Born in Toronto, Ontario.

One of the things that Bev, who had been trained as a nurse, perfected after her marriage to her husband, Doug, who is a neurosurgeon, and the arrival of their children, was how to juggle more than one responsibility at a time. In part from necessity because of Doug's extended hours, Bev survived by being organized and having a reliable schedule to follow. These essential skills assisted her tremendously when she turned her attention to local politics, first as a campaign manager in 1974, as president of her resident's association from 1974 to 1984, then as the aldermanic candidate in North York in 1976.

Bev has been involved in a life-long struggle against racism and consequently was a founding member of the Urban Alliance on Race Relations and served on it's Board and Executive from 1975 to 1981. She was a Commissioner with the Ontario Human Rights Commission from 1979 to 1985 and had been appointed to the Ontario Status of Women Council. From 1985 to 1988, she served on the North York Mayor's Committee on Community, Race and Ethnic Relations. Bev is Chair of the Council Action Committee to Combat Racism, the Race Relations Working Group on Metropolitan Toronto Delivery of Children's Services and she is the Chair of the Black Educator's Working Group.

Bev has been representing North York Centre South since 1988 and previously she served one term on the Council of the City of North York. Her political interests include involvement in more than twenty committees. Bev has been awarded the Mayor' Certificate of Recognition (1974) , the Canada Day Achievement Award (1992) and the Jamaican-Canadian Women's Committee Certificate of Appreciation (1993). Her dedication to making changes in the local political arena has benefitted North York area residents and set an example for other municipalities.

MAIRUTH SARSFIELD: Writer, Communicator, Television Host, Statesperson, Environmentalist, Collector. Born on March 6, 1930 in Montreal, Quebec.

Sharing her parents love of the written word and languages, Mairuth's entry into Journalism at Colombia University was supported by her parents, Edgar and Anne Packwood, the founders of one of Montreal's first Black newspapers. Initially Mairuth wrote children's stories inspired by her children, Jennifer and Jeremy, including "How Santa Clause Nearly Lost His Toys". Entering the fashion industry briefly as a promoter, she hosted 2 television shows, Montreal's "Hourglass" and an Ottawa children's show, "Sandbox." Mairuth had succeeded in coordinating the "People Tree", a communications centre, at Expo '67 in Montreal, she was invited to coordinate the them, "Discovery", for the Canadian Pavilion of Expo '70 in Osaka, Japan, making Mairuth the highest-placed woman in Canada's creative field. The theme attempted to convey what is Canadian and was a "chance for the visual arts to portray an intangible thing, the spirit of a people". The award-winning pavilion designed by Arthur Erikson was one of the first exhibits to use multiple screens for viewing an array of images simultaneously.

Joining External Affairs of the Federal Civil Service, Mairuth's competence in communications was noticed by the United Nations. In 1979 Mairuth accepted a post in Nairobi, Kenya as the Assistant Director of International Information for the United Nations Environment Programme. She created and promoted the best environmental theme and program of the year, "For Every Child a Tree" which resulted in 100,000 trees being planted in Kenya alone and which involved children around the world in meaningful environmental activities. Her knowledge and enthusiasm about environmental issues during a 1983 Cleveland presentation lead the Major and the National Council of Negro Women to declare October 22nd as "Mairuth Sarsfield Day".

In Canada, she has received the Ordre National du Quebec on June 26, 1985. Mairuth is on the Board of CBC, Carleton University, National Film Board and is President of MATCH International. She co-hosts TV Ontario's "The Senior Report" and has founded with her husband Dominick and sister Lucille the "Equatoria Collection" of books modelled on the Schomberg Collection of New York.

DR. GLENDA SIMMS: Psychologist, Educator, Feminist. Born in Jamaica, West Indies.

Having received her early education and teacher training in Jamaica, Glenda started a degree in education at the University of Alberta upon her arrival in 1971 with her family to Calgary. She began her teaching career with Native children in Fort Chipewyan in northern Alberta. Glenda completed her studies for a Master of Education in 1976 while managing her home and her children. She taught in the Native education department of the University of Regina and was the Supervisor of race and ethnic relations with the Regina Public School Board while completing her Doctorate granted in 1985. She then taught Native Canadian education and Educational Psychology at Nipissing University College in North Bay.

Glenda was appointed President and Chief Executive Officer of the Canadian Advisory Council on the Status of Women in 1990. She manages a budget of $3.5 million. Her proudest achievement was the national symposium for young women held in 1992 called "Widening the Circle", the first such event of its kind. They produced video presentations, one of which called "Grandmother, Mother and Me" is a six part series focussing on the lives of Canadian women from different ethnic backgrounds. The issues of racism, feminism and multiculturalism are addressed through Glenda's work with the CACSW.

Glenda is doing everything she can to improve the conditions of women in her native Jamaica, by conducting workshops with government administrators and with grass-root women's organizations. She feels that there is a lot that Canadian women can do in international development work to make a difference. For her dedication and purposeful work, Glenda has been awarded the Distinguished Alumni Award from the University of Alberta.

BETTY SIMPSON: Co-founder of the North American Black Historical Museum. Born in Colchester South (near Windsor, Ontario).

When Betty married Melvin "Mac" Simpson, a floral designer and musician, she became aware of his many interests and of his dream to see a museum of Black History erected in the Amherstburg area. In 1979, they started to work seriously on making his dream a reality , and when they were finished, the African Methodist Episcopal Church, a new building, and a log cabin combined to form the museum. Betty continues to volunteer her time to the museum even now that Mac has died. She is keeping his dream alive while at the same time keeping alive another chapter in the history of Amherstburg and of Canada. Attracting visitors from across Canada and the United States, the museum represents the idea of freedom, the heritage of people of African descent and sheds light in a meaningful way on the previously ignored contributions of Blacks in Canada.

Betty represents the commitment, determination and dedication of people to make a difference. While others, such as Helen Smith in St. Catharines, Wilma Morrison in Niagara Falls and the late Arlie Robbins in North Buxton, have volunteered as coordinator , guide and reference source at their respective museum/historic sites, it is Betty who has received a Canada 125 Medal for her dedication in keeping the North American Historical Museum going.

FLORENCE SMITH-BAULD: Teacher and Community Volunteer. Born in Weymouth Falls, Nova Scotia.

Florence is the type of teacher who students remember long after being in her class. Maybe her early experience of being among the few Black students at her school or her understanding of independent learning when she took a home study course in music helped her to be sensitive to others and to make learning serious but fun. Qualified to teach piano privately, Florence was approached to teach all subjects in the Black schools of Nova Scotia and she prepared for teaching by taking a summer program at the Provincial Normal School. Florence taught in a one-room school, and so impressed the school inspector with her dedication and efficiency that she was given a bursary to attend school herself in order to receive her teaching qualifications by 1957. By 1972, Florence was awarded a citation to recognize her outstanding volunteer work organizing branches of the Red Cross Youth wing for 15 years. Florence's commitment to excellence made her feel it was important to obtain a certificate allowing her to teach music, which she loves, in the public schools of Nova Scotia. Although presently retired, Florence has devoted all of her life to improving the condition of her students, and her community. She was on the Board of the Black Cultural Centre, assisted with the work of her church, founded the Black Professional Women's Group and was the president of the Black Educators Association.

To honour her contributions, Florence has been presented with several awards, including plaques from the Victoria Road United Baptist Church, a YWCA award for her outstanding contribution in addressing the status of women in the community, and certificates from the Congress of Black Women of Canada, Black Educator's Group, and the Black Cultural Centre.

ALMETA SPEAKS: Film Producer, Writer, Singer, Beautician. Born in Reidsville, North Carolina.

Almeta began singing gospel at home with her family and then on a Sunday morning radio program with her sisters when she was 13. Later trained to be a hairdresser, Almeta moved to New York City to expand her beautician ability but found that she needed more stimulation and more money than this work could provide. So, as a 21 year old, she began to sing with an accompaniest, but soon forged out a solo act. After two years of performing gospel-inspired blues in restaurants and clubs, Almeta was invited to Toronto in 1964 for a 2 week job at the Castle George, a stint that lasted 11 months.

Almeta identifies early blues singers as the chroniclers of the Black community in North America. She feels that they "expressed the fundamental experiences of being Black - the conditions, issues, concerns of the time, as well as our joys and sadness." Almeta sees her interest and talents as expressing the history of the Black community whether she is singing the blues, writing a book or working on a television show. "I'm really only doing the same thing all the time."

By 1971, Almeta had moved to Vancouver, in part to perform at the Princess Louise, but also to continue to do research on the contributions of Black people to the development of Canada. This interest had prompted Almeta to accept bookings in areas where she wished to do research, such as Dresden, with its association with Josiah Henson, Halifax with its community of Africville, Saint John, with its settlement at Loch Lomond and Vancouver, with the Salt Spring Island community. The opportunity to acquire formal education in the study of people came when Almeta was awarded a Regents scholarship which was a special fund for minorities from the University of California in San Diego. Almeta began to prepare for her actual college days by limiting her performances. Not following the advice of her faculty advisor to reduce her course selections, Almeta started in January 1975 and graduated in June 1978 with degrees in sociology, communications, with a minor in music. Noting the absence of programming for, about or by Blacks, Almeta demanded that the public broadcasting station do so, and she became the host of a weekly musical special called "Celebrate Life" after her grant applications and plans for the show were approved. A later show, "Almeta Speaks With", won a production of historical/cultural series Emmy in 1978. When Almeta decided to leave San Diego to go on tour for research , lecture and performance purposes, using Toronto as a base, she was leaving behind her position as Executive Director and Producer of the Office of Ethnic Programs for KPBS television in San Diego.

Now president of her own company, "Almeta Speaks Productions Inc.," which manages Almeta's vocal albums and projects, Almeta has produced a television mini-series , "Hymn to Freedom" based on the history of people of African descent in Canada as represented by four families. Almeta is leading the way to greater cultural awareness and understanding through her dynamic personality and her expressions in song, word or film.

LENETTA TYLER: Universal Woman, Wife and Mother. Born in New Brunswick.

Lenetta does not see herself as being worthy of mention, but to those who know her, she is held in high esteem. All women who are pursuing positive and helpful pursuits that assist in the growth of the people they influence could be identified as people who are making a positive contribution to society. Lenetta is included as a representative of all Black women who have done what they could to make a difference. All positive activities, from providing a warm and nurturing environment for their children to making policy decisions affecting society in general contribute to positive developments whether in the home or in the nation. We can all "lead the way in our own way", by using the skills, education, position and opportunities that uniquely exist for each one of us to the best of our ability.

Married to Seymore Tyler, a soldier, railwayman and farmer, Lenetta joined her husband in farming near the Ripples/Minto area of New Brunswick after he closed the trucking business he had started in Saint John. They had three daughters and four sons and 27 grandchildren and 10 great-grandchildren.

Seymore had played in the Saint John Brass Band and organized the first Boy Scout Bugle Band in Saint John. Seymore enlisted in the No. 2 Construction Battalion, the only Black Canadian battalion to serve in World War I. Though never engaged in combat, one of their responsibilities was to locate and diffuse land mines. After returning to New Brunswick, he maintained his ties to the military by belonging to the Carleton-York Regiment which was later named part of the first regiment to be sent oversees at the start of World War II, with Bugle Sergeant Tyler. He was sent home in 1941, because his leg was broken in 7 places during a bombing attack in the Battle of Britain. When he recovered, he became a railway porter, until 1959, travelling from Saint John to Boston, Montreal, Toronto and Vancouver.

Clearly, while Seymore was away at war or travelling because of his job, Lenetta had to survive and ensure that her children were fed and properly cared for, so the bulk of the responsibility for managing the farm or the home and the children was left for her. Her husband, Seymore, was awarded the Silver Bugle in 1939 and a citation in recognition of his service to the Number 2 Construction Battalion in 1983, but for her efforts, Lenetta has received no public awards. And, thousands of women perform the real hard, often tedious tasks of keeping their families going, often while working outside of their homes as well.

PORTIA WHITE: World Class Singer, Contralto. Born on June 24, 1911 in Halifax and died on February, 13, 1968, in Toronto.

The daughter of an American-born Baptist minister, who became the only Black Canadian chaplain with the British forces during World War 1, Portia began singing in her father's church choir when she was 6-years old. One of ten children, the family often made up the entire choir, so clearly, music was a strong part of their lives. When Portia was 8-years old, she appeared in a music festival with her sister singing excerpts from "Lucia". Portia went on to win many prizes for music and had decided to become a concert singer while in high school. To support her dream, she accepted a position as a teacher, some eighteen miles from Halifax, to earn money to pay for her voice lessons, but she had to walk 3 miles each way just to get to the train that would take her into Halifax.

People began to hear about her talent and she was invited to sing throughout the area. She won first prize at four different festivals for mezzo-soprano solo, three of these wins in consecutive years, which resulted in her being awarded the silver cup, now permanently housed in the Black Cultural Centre of Dartmouth. An audition was arranged for her with Dr. Ernesto Vinci , head of the vocal department of the Halifax Conservatory of Music. He was so impressed with her voice that she was awarded a Halifax Ladies Musical Club scholarship, in 1939. Under Vinci's training, she changed from the mezzo to the contralto range, and again so impressed Dr. Edith Read, principle of Branksome Hall, in Toronto, that she arranged a concert in Toronto in November 1941 for Portia which was given glowing reviews. With the promise of support by her patrons, Portia resigned from teaching to concentrate on her studies. The government of Nova Scotia established a Portia White Trust to assist her financially.

Dr. Read again intervened to give Portia assistance: she arranged an audition for Portia with Edward Johnson, General Manager of the Metropolitan Opera in New York. After many successful Canadian engagements, Portia entered the international spotlight on March 13, 1944 at New York's Town Hall. This triumphant concert lead to more tours across the United States; by 1946, the Caribbean, South America, Central America; by 1948, England and France. Portia won many awards for her remarkable ability including the distinguished Cultural Medal of the Isthmanian Negro Congress in Panama City. Portia's talent was often compared to Marion Anderson, the famous American singer.

After 1955, Portia lived in Toronto in semi-retirement, teaching and coaching in traditional and contemporary music and in 1964, she sang for Queen Elizabeth and Prince Philip at the opening of the Confederation Centre in Charlottetown, P.E.I.. The sheer excellence of her voice, the intelligence of her interpretations and the nature of her personality combined to make Portia a living legend.

DR. DOROTHY WILLS: Educator and Social Worker. Born on March 16, 1933 in Dominica, West Indies.

Dorothy came to Halifax to study at Mount Saint Vincent University after completing high school in Grenada and secretarial training in Barbados. She received the Silver Medal for her academic excellence in completing her B. Sc., the first of many honours and distinctions. She married Roland Wills of Nigeria, and the couple settled in Montreal to raise their two children. Dorothy received her Master of Social Work degree from McGill University in 1966 followed by a specialist teaching diploma in

1969, a Master of Arts degree in 1977 and a Ph.D. in Education by 1979. An additional, honorary degree of LL. D. was conferred on her in 1989 by Concordia University.

Dorothy has worked as a court stenographer for the government of Dominica; counselled the physically challenged, the aged and troubled youth as a social worker; taught on Mohawk territories, at high school, community college and at the university level where Dorothy has been on the faculty of Vanier College since 1971. She has also been a member of the Immigration and Refugee Board of Canada since 1988. Her commitment to ensuring that all people are free or treated equally, has made her value the search and discussion about the achievements of Blacks in Canada and around the world.

Dorothy's list of community involvements is just as significant as her academic achievements: from 1967 to 1969, she was the Director of the Negro Community Centre of Montreal; and from 1969 to 1971 she was the first Black member of the Board of Directors of the Federation of Catholic Charities. She served as President of the Negro Citizenship Association and was a founding member of the National Black Coalition of Canada. Dorothy has served as the Executive Director of the Quebec Board of Black Educators and was a member of the Canadian Multiculturalism Council. Dorothy has been appointed to numerous municipal, provincial and federal committees, including the Comite Consultatif de Relations Interculturelles of Montreal, and she was the coordinator of Canada's delegation to the Festival of Arts and Culture in Lagos, Nigeria.

Other awards that Dorothy has received include the Mount Saint Vincent University Alumni Jubilee Award of Distinction, the National Black Coalition of Canada Gold Award for Community Service, the Congress of Black Women Award for educational programs, the Martin Luther King Jr. Achievement Award, the Order of Canada and the Minister's Award for Excellence in Race Relations. Dorothy has used her intelligence, her energy and her commitment to a better society to make changes affecting us all.

CAROLYN WILSON: Community Worker, Counsellor. Born in Collingwood, Ontario.

One of the myths of the Underground Railroad is that freedom-seekers only settled in border towns. But Carolyn is the ninth generation of her family to come from this area of Ontario. The daughter of Herbert and Yvonne (Sheffield) Wilson, Carolyn with her sister and brother, Sylvia and Herbert, developed a commitment to helping people, initially through their church and through working at Sheffield's Cedar Inn, an early Black restaurant, and Sheffield's Tent and Trailer Park, both family owned and operated.

At church, she began singing duets with Sylvia and they continue to work together now that Carolyn is the Music Director of the Heritage Community Songsters and the Methodist Gospel Choir, which Carolyn founded over 20 years ago, while Sylvia is a Director and Pianist.

Carolyn has travelled with her choirs, and has also travelled across Canada with the thousand children she trained in the Starlite Majorette Corp during her teens. She has been honoured by the Order of the Eastern Star Prince Hall, a Black fraternal organization, and she received the Matron of the Year Award in 1979 for her contributions in office. Carolyn has initiated several community programs through the C.S. Wilson Centre , the centre also founded by Carolyn 20 years ago, to develop positive attitudes among all citizens. She acts as an advocate for her multicultural students

Along with family members and the Pioneer Cemetery Committee, Carolyn was able to locate the burial place of her ancestors in the Flesherton area of Artemesia Township. The discovery lead to the honouring of the site with a ceremony and plaque by the Lieutenant Governor of Ontario. Not only did the discovery have personal meaning for Carolyn and her family but also it was more evidence to show that Blacks cleared and settled in the area prior to European settlement. In Collingwood, the Sheffield establishments have been restructured to promote the Black History, Cultural and Education Museum and Carolyn works with her uncle, Howard Sheffield, to promote the contributions of these early Black pioneers through presentations locally and abroad.

Carolyn has received many public-speaking and music awards and certificates and she received the 125th Canada Anniversary Medal for her activities. Both Carolyn and her sister, Sylvia, have been recognized with the Order of Collingwood for making a difference to so many people.

SELECTED FIRSTS OF BLACK WOMEN IN CANADA

Mrs Wilson Abbott: Founded the first Black women's mutual aid group, the Queen Victoria Benevolent Society, 1840, in Toronto.

Angelique: One of the first Black women to be executed, for arson in her attempt to seek her freedom, 1734, in Montreal.

Zanana Akande: First Black woman member of the Provincial Parliament, Ontario.

Lena Anderson: Honoured counsellor of immigrant women in Winnipeg.

Virnetta Anderson: Dedicated community worker in Calgary.

Rosetta Amos: Proprietor of the first soul food restaurant, 1891, in Toronto.

Miss O. T. Augusta: Early Toronto businesswoman, in dry goods and dress making

Jean Augustine: First chairperson, Metropolitan Toronto Housing Authority.

Reverend Addie Aylestock: First Black woman ordained in Canada, 1951.

Marian Barnes: Owner of early restaurant in Hamil ton, 1851.

Dr. Carrie Best: Founder and editor of The *Clarion* and received the Order of Canada.

Violet Blackman: founding member of the United Negro Credit Union, 1940s, in Toronto.

Jestina Blake-Hill: Storyteller in Regina and President of the Congress of Black Women of Canada.

Madame Leona Brewton: First Black beauty shop owner in Toronto, in 1929: invented reflector: organizer of Toronto Young Men's Bible Class.

Paola Brown: Led a protest in 1837 against the arrest of Jesse Happy, fugitive slave, in Hamilton.

Dr. Rosemary Brown: First member of the Legislative Assembly of British Columbia.

Rosetta Cadogan: Nursing educator and advocate for Sickle Cell Survivors, in Montreal.

Evangeline Cain-Grant: First Black woman to graduate in Law from North Preston, Nova Scotia.

Canadian Negro Women's Association: First celebration of Negro History Week in 1958.

Linda Carter: One of the first international top models of Toronto.

Chloe Cooley: Her 1793 kidnapping and re-enslavement prompted Lieutenant-Governor Simcoe to work towards the abolition of slavery in Upper Canada, 1793.

Senator Ann Cools: First Black woman appointed to the Senate in January 13, 1984.

Rita Cox: Assembled first and largest Black Heritage/ West Indian collection in Toronto Public Library system.

Jean Daniels: Founder of the Library of Black Literature, 1968, in Toronto.

Lorelle Dart: Renowned choir director and musician in North York.

Rosey Edeh: 1988 Quebec Hopeful Athlete of the Year in 400 m hurdles and 400 m.

Dr. Eniz Elliston: Scarborough educator responsible for many multicultural policies.

Fran Endicott: Educator and first Black woman to head the Ontario Human Rights Commission.

Reba Fleming: Organized "Good Friends" at First Baptist Church, Toronto.

Rose Fortune: First Black police woman, 1825, Annapolis Royal.

Mesha Gosman: Internationally recognized gospel singer.

Penelope Hodge: Historian of First Baptist Church in Toronto.

Mitzie Hunter: Young entrepreneur, founded model and talent agency, 1992.

Angela Issajenko: Sprinter, 100 m and 200 m, received the Order of Canada in 1985.

Dr. June James: One of the first Black women allergists in Winnipeg.

Gwen Barton Jenkins: First Black woman in Nova Scotia to graduate from a Canadian nursing school.

Gwen Johnston: Co-founder with her husband of the Toronto's first bookstore dedicated to books by and about people of African descent, established in 1968.

Dorothy Jones: First Black woman to be National president for the Canadian Operation Research Society.

Lona Joseph: Founder and director of Black Family Association Camp in Montreal, 1993.

Dr. Alfreda (Simons) Kartha: Founding member and chairperson of the Ontario Universities Coalition for Education in Health Care of the Elderly.

Sandra Levy: CIAU All-Canadian in 1985-1989, 1992 and 1993.

Corinth Lewis: Edmonton teacher honoured by Alberta Teachers' Association in 1993.

Daurene Lewis: First Black woman mayor, Annapolis Royal.

Susan Libertis: Early herbalist in Collingwood, 1835.

Kay Livingstone: Founder of Canadian Negro Women's Association, 1951.

Phyllis Marshall: Actress in CBC's first television variety show, 1951.

Mattie Mayes: Maidstone, Saskatchewan, pioneer, born a slave in the U.S.

Lena O'ree: Pianist, playing for the first television show in New Brunswick in the 1950s.

Anne Packwood: Longest serving foster parent in Montreal, by 1966.

Jean Parris: President, Congress of Black Women in Montreal.

Mariene Philip Norbese; One of the first Black Canadian novelists, who wrote *Harriet's Daughter* in 1980s.

Sophia Pooley: First Black woman slave in southern Ontario.

Thelma Powell-Brown: Founder and director of Powell-Brown Therapeutic Nursery School, 1964, in Toronto.

Claire Prieto: Filmmaker noted for "Home to Buxton" and "Older, Stronger, Wiser".

Michelin Rawlins: First Black woman, Ontario Court Bench, Judge, 1992.

Bernice Redmon: First Canadian-born nurse from Ontario to work n Public Health.

Elizabeth Maria Duvall Rolling: Piano accompanist for nickelodeon and leading dressmaker in Barrie, in the early 1900s.

Lillian Rutherford: Founder of Phyliis Wheately Art Club, 1922, which developed into the Negro Theatre Guild of Montreal.

Irene Reddick: First Black principal in Nova Scotia.

Mairuth Sarsfield: Highest ranking Black woman in Canada's communications field.

Kathy Searles: Dedicated community organizer in Toronto.

Mary Ann Shadd: First Black woman publisher in North America; the publisher and founder of the first anti-slavery newspaper; first Black woman to complete law degree at Howard University; and first Black woman paid as a recruitment officer.

Dr. Glenda Simms: First Black woman to head the Canadian Advisory Council on the Status of Women.

Ola Skanks: Early African heritage dancer and designer in Toronto in the 1960s.

Eva Smith: Diligent worker with the Black youth in Toronto from the 1960s to 1994.

Corinne Sparks: One of the first Black women to be a judge in Nova Scotia.

Sylvia Sweeney: Film producer and director, she is well known for her film, "In the Key of Oscar".

Madeline Symonds: First Black to graduate from the Provincial Normal College in Nova Scotia, 1927.

Harriet Tubman: Conductor on the Underground Railroad; the only woman to have led a military attack in North American history, during the American Civil War.

Dr. Maxine Tynes: One of the first Black Canadian poets, published in 1987, and awarded the People's Poet of Canada Award in 1988.

Amanda "Nettie" Janet Ware: Pioneer of Alberta, born in 1893 and daughter of the first Black cowboy, John Ware.

Stella Umeh: National Team member for Gymnastics since 1988.

Janice Vandyke: Writer of children's books, including *Like Little Leaves*, published in 1973, from Windsor.

Nerene Virgin: Television host and actress.

Clotida Yakimchuk: First Black woman to preside over 9600 members of the Registered Nurses Association of Nova Scotia.

FURTHER READING

Bearden, Jim and Butler, Linda Jean. *The Life and Times of Mary Ann Shadd Cary*. Toronto: New Canada Press, 1977.

Bentley, Judith. *Harriet Tubman*. New York: Franklin Watts, 1990.

Bertley, Leo. *Canada and It's People of African Descent*. Pierrefonds, Quebec: Bilongo Publishers, 1977.

Best, Dr. Carrie. *The Lonesome Road: The Autobiography of Carrie M. Best.* New Glasgow: Clarion Publishing Co. Ltd., 1977.

Bradford, Sarah. *Scenes in the Life of Harriet Tubman*. 1869.

Bramble, Linda. *Black Fugitive Slaves in Early Canada*. 1989.

Brown, Hallie. *Homespun Heroines and Other Women of Distinction*. Aldine Press, 1926.

Brown, Rosemary. *Being Brown: A Very Public Life*. Toronto: Ballantine Books, 1989.

Clairmont, Donald H. and Magill, Dennis W. *Africville: The Life and Death of a Canadian Community*. Toronto: Canadian Scholars Press, 1974.

Conrad, Earl. *Harriet Tubman*. New York: P. Eriksson Press, 1943.

D'Oyley, E.F. and Braithwaite, R. *Women of Our Times*. By the Canadian Negro Women's Association for the National Congress of Black Women, Toronto: Sheppard & Sears, 1973.

Hill, Daniel. *The Freedom-Seekers: Blacks in Early Canada.* Toronto: The Book Society of Canada Ltd., 1981.

Hill, Lawrence. *Trials and Triumphs: The Story of African-Canadians*. Toronto: Umbrella Press, 1993.

Kilian, Crawford. *Go Do Some Great Thing: The Black Pioneers of British Columbia*. Vancouver: Douglas and McIntyre, 1978.

Landon, Fred. "The Negro Migration to Canada, After the Passing of the Fugitive Slave Act," in *Journal of Negro History*, 5 (1920), pages 437-447.

MacDonald, Cheryl. "Mary Ann Shadd in Canada - Last Stop on the Underground Railroad," in *The Beaver*. February/March, 1990.

OECA. *Identity: The Black Experience in Canada.* Toronto, 1979.

Ontario Ministry of Citizenship and Culture. *An Enduring Heritage, Black Contributions to Early Ontario.* Toronto: Dundurn Press, 1984.

Petry, Ann. *Harriet Tubman - Conductor on the Underground Railroad.*New York: Thomas Y. Crowell Company.

Ripley, C. P., ed. *The Black Abolitionist Papers, Vol. II, Canada 1830-1865.* Chapel Hill: University of Carolina Press, 1986.

Ross, Sandi. *Into the Mainstream*, for ACTRA. Toronto, 1992.

Ruck, Calvin W. *Black Battalion: 1916-1920, Canada's Best Kept Military Secret.* Halifax: Nimbus Publishing, 1987.

Shadd, Mary Ann. *A Plea for Emigration or Notes on Canada West.* Detroit: printed by George W. Pattison, 1852.

Simpson, D.G. "Negroes in Ontario from Early Times to 1870". Unpublished Ph.D. Thesis, University of Western Ontario, 1971.

Spray, W.A. *Blacks in New Brunswick*. Fredericton: New Brunswick Press, 1972.

Still, William. *The Underground Railroad*. Philadelphia: People's Publishing, 1879.

Talbot, Carol. *Growing Up Black in Canada*. Toronto: Williams-Wallace, 1984.

Thompson, Colin. *Blacks in Deep Snow: Black Pioneers in Canada*. Don Mills: J.M. Dent, 1979.

Tulloch, Headley. *Black Canadians: A Long Line of Fighters*. Toronto: N.C. Press Ltd., 1980.

Walls, Bryan E. *The Road that Led to Somewhere*. Windsor: Olive Publishing Company, 1980.

Winks, Robin. *The Blacks in Canada: A History*. Montreal: McGill-Queens Press, 1971.

INDEX

PICTURE CREDITS

The cooperation of persons and organizations in providing photographs for reproduction in the book is gratefully appreciated .

Page 5: The Charles L. Blockson Afro-American Collection, Temple University; Page 7: Ontario Black History Society; Page 8: *map*, Stephen Taylor; Page 9: Ontario Black History Society; Page 10: *top*, Ontario Black History Society; *bottom*, (Harriet Tubman) St. Catharines Historical Museum, N 8969; Page 12: Gwen Robinson; Page 13: *map*, Stephen Taylor; Page 14: Mrs. E. Williams, The Harriet Tubman Home, 180 South St., Auburn, New York; Page 15: The Harriet Tubman Home, 180 South St., Auburn, New York; Page 16: both pictures, Raleigh Township Centennial Museum Historic Black Canadian Settlement, North Buxton, Ontario; Page 17: Gwen Robinson; Page 18: Henry Bibb, Metropolitan Toronto Reference Library, 963, C 1/31; *Voice of the Fugitive*, Metropolitan Toronto Reference Library, 963 C 1/50; Page 19: North American Black Historical Museum, Amherstburg, Ontario; Page 20: Ontario Black History Society; Page 22: Shadd Family Tree, Raleigh Township Centennial Museum Historic Black Canadian Settlement, North Buxton, Ontario; Page 23: Raleigh Township Centennial Museum Historic Black Canadian Settlement, North Buxton, Ontario; Page 25: Black Cultural Centre for Nova Scotia, Dartmouth, Nova Scotia; Page 28: Rosemary Sadlier; Page 31: Rosemary Sadlier; Page 33: The Ontario Human Rights Commission; Pages 39, 40, 42, 43, 44: Sylvia Sweeney; Page 47: The National Film Board, from "In the Key of Oscar".